Songs

Under the greenwood tree   Act III   sc. 5
Blow, blow,   Act. II Sc 7
What shall he have that killed the deer
                                    IV. sc. 8

It was a lover & his lass   Act V   sc. 3
Allotted to Hymen   Act V   sc. 4

Euphues Golden Legacie.

Found after his death in his Cell at
SILEXEDRA.

Bequeathed to PHILAVTVS Sonnes,
nursed vp with their Father in
ENGLAND

Fetcht from the Canaries, by T. L., Gent.

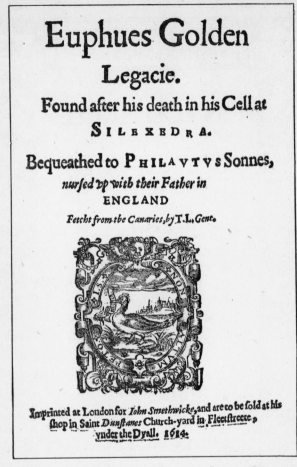

Imprinted at London for *Iohn Smethwicke*, and are to be sold at his
shop in Saint *Dunstanes* Church-yard in Fleetstreete,
vnder the Dyall. 1612.

FACSIMILE OF TITLE-PAGE, EUPHUES GOLDEN LEGACIE,
BLACK-LETTER EDITION

Reproduced from the copy in the Boston Public Library

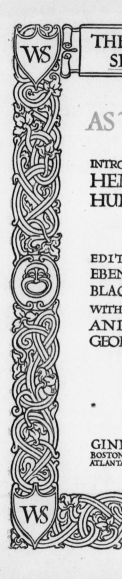

THE NEW HUDSON SHAKESPEARE

AS YOU LIKE IT

INTRODUCTION AND NOTES BY
**HENRY NORMAN
HUDSON, LL·D·**

EDITED AND REVISED BY
**EBENEZER CHARLTON
BLACK LL·D· (GLASGOW)**
WITH THE COÖPERATION OF
**ANDREW JACKSON
GEORGE L·TT·D·(AMHERST)**

GINN AND COMPANY
BOSTON NEW YORK CHICAGO LONDON
ATLANTA DALLAS COLUMBUS SAN FRANCISCO

PREFACE

Exclusive of changes in spelling, punctuation, and stage directions, only seven variations from the text of the First Folio occur in the text of this edition of *As You Like It*. These variations are such corrections as were made either in the later seventeenth century Folios or in Rowe's octavo editions of 1709 and 1714. These corrections and variations, with the more important suggested emendations of later editors, are indicated in the textual notes. The only omissions are such passages as are out of place in a school edition.

The spelling and the punctuation of the text are modern, except in the case of verb terminations in *-ed*, which, when the *e* is silent, are printed with the apostrophe in its place. This is the general usage in the First Folio. Modern spelling has to a certain extent been followed in the text variants; but the original spelling has been retained wherever its peculiarities have been the basis for important textual criticism and emendation.

With regard to the general plan of this revision of Hudson's Shakespeare, Professor W. P. Trent, of Columbia University, has offered valuable suggestions and given important advice.

SEPTEMBER 1, 1906

CONTENTS

INTRODUCTION

THE TEXT

INTRODUCTION

NOTE. In citations from Shakespeare's plays and nondramatic poems the numbering has reference to the Globe edition, except in the case of this play, where the reference is to this edition.

I. SOURCES

The story-theme of a quarrel between brothers leading to strange and unexpected results is common to all literature. The story of Cain and Abel, with unending variations, is universal. An interesting modification of this theme — when a jealous elder brother keeps a younger out of his inheritance, and the younger becomes prosperous in the teeth of all difficulties and obstacles — is in the ancient Egyptian *Tale of Two Brothers*[1] and in the *Genesis* narrative of Joseph and his brethren; it is, with significant changes, the framework of the parable of the Prodigal Son. *As You Like It* is a variant and a development of this world-old and universal story-theme, with elements and color that come from the soil and atmosphere of the England of Robin Hood ballads and Elizabethan pastoral.

THE MAIN STORY

1. *The Tale of Gamelyn.* The earliest form of the *As You Like It* story in English literature is *The Tale of Gamelyn*, a vigorous ballad-epic of nine hundred and two

[1] For similar stories in different literatures, see A. Lang's *Myth, Ritual, and Religion.*

lines in northern dialect. This poem, which philology and story-development connect with the Anglo-Danish cycle of legends to which *Havelok the Dane* and *Hamlet* belong, seems to have been in Chaucer's possession, and it was probably his plan to work it over for use in *The Canterbury Tales*. After his death it was found inserted among manuscripts of *The Canterbury Tales* immediately after the fragment of *The Coke's (Cook's) Tale*. "A late hand, in the Harl. MS. 7334, has scribbled above it—'The Coke's Tale of Gamelyn'; whence the blunder arose of connecting it with the Cook."—Skeat.

In *The Tale of Gamelyn* are many of the incidents of *As You Like It*. The story turns upon the neglect and abuse of a youngest brother by an eldest; and a violent quarrel, a wrestling match, the rescue of the youngest brother by an old retainer called Adam, and an escape to forest depths are inwoven, but there is no thread of love in the weaving.

2. *Robin Hood Ballads and Plays.* Story, treatment, and nomenclature connect *The Tale of Gamelyn* also with the Robin Hood ballad cycle, Gamelyn being in all probability identical with 'Young Gamwell' of the ballad *Robin Hood Newly Revived:*

> " But thou art a cousin of Robin Hood's then?
>   The sooner we should have done":
> "As I hope to be sav'd," the stranger then said,
>   "I am his own sister's son."

Compare also "Gamble Gold of the gay green woods" in the ballad *The Bold Pedlar and Robin Hood*. Apart from *The Tale of Gamelyn* as a link between Robin Hood lore and *As You Like It*, we find Shakespeare himself giving a significant source-hint in I, i, 105-107: "They say he is already in the forest of Arden, and a many merry men with him; and there they live like the old Robin Hood of England." There is evidence that from the beginning of the fifteenth century Robin Hood, Maid Marian, and their companions were the subject of popular dramatic performances and rustic pageants,[1] and thus pastoralism and the wild wood atmosphere grew up with the English drama, and towards the close of the sixteenth century found expression in such plays as *The Downfall of Robert, Earl of Huntington*, by Anthony Munday, *The Death of Robert, Earl of Huntington*, by Munday and Henry Chettle, and *George-a-Greene, the Pinner of Wakefield*, often attributed to Robert Greene.

3. *Lodge's Rosalynde*. *The Tale of Gamelyn* was not printed until the eighteenth century, but there is no doubt that manuscript copies were in circulation in the sixteenth; and upon the story as found in one of these manuscript versions, Thomas Lodge founded his prose romance, *Rosalynde. Euphues Golden Legacie: found after his death in his Cell at Silexedra. Bequeathed to Philautus sonnes noursed up with their father in England. Fetcht from the Canaries. By T. L. Gent. London, Imprinted by Thomas Orwin for T. G. and John Busbie. 1590.* The popularity of Lodge's *Rosalynde* is shown by its having been reprinted again and again between 1590 and 1640, some of the later editions omitting 'Rosalynde' from the title.[2] This success was due to the skill

---

[1] See "Robin Hood Plays" in Manly's *Specimens of the Pre-Shakespearean Drama*, I, 279–288, Ginn & Company, 1900. See also Gayley's "An Historical View of English Comedy," XL–XLI, *Representative English Comedies*, The Macmillan Company, 1903.

[2] See the facsimile of the title-page of the black-letter copy in the Boston Public Library given as the frontispiece of this edition.

with which Lodge in his redaction of the sturdy old story
combined the euphuistic diction and manner that Lyly had
made fashionable from 1580 to 1590 and the courtly pastoralism which the genius of Spenser and Sidney made so
strong a literary influence during the next decade. After
the posthumous publication of the *Arcadia* in 1590, pastoralism became the very breath of the English court and literary life ; it influenced every one. " The mere fact that a
man was writing verse was sufficient to metamorphose him
for the time into a shepherd, and the persons about him
into shepherds and shepherdesses. The very name ' shepherd ' became a synonym for ' poet.' " — Masson.

While it is a disputed question, and likely to remain so,
whether Shakespeare ever read *The Tale of Gamelyn*,[1] it is
beyond a doubt that *Rosalynde* is the immediate source of
the plot of *As You Like It*. In the play linger a few char-
acteristic euphuisms in the form of classical allusions, ' pul-
pit employment' of fictitious natural history as in II, i, 12–14,
alliteration and antithesis in the sentence structure ; and we
have certain artificial pastoral conventions of the Renaissance
in the wooing of Silvius and Phebe, the disguise of Rosalind,
the hunting scene, etc., though these are blended with the
bracing air of English country life under the greenwood tree.
But it is in the incidents of the narrative that Shakespeare
appropriated so much from *Rosalynde*, and to appreciate
fully his use of this material, it is necessary to compare the
romance and the drama scene by scene.[2] Only in this way

[1] See articles by Delius (*Shakespeare Jahrbuch*, VI, 226), Zupitza
(*Shakespeare Jahrbuch*, XXI, 69), and Stone (*New Shakspere Society
Transactions*, 1880–1886, p. 277).

[2] The complete text of *Rosalynde* is given in Hazlitt's *Shakespeare's Library*, Vol. II, 1875.

can be understood the judgment and art with which Shakespeare used the borrowed matter. In no one of his comedies
indeed has he borrowed more freely; nor is there any
wherein he has enriched his borrowings more liberally from
the glory of his own genius. To appreciate his wisdom as
shown in what he left unused, one must read the whole of
Lodge's romance. In that work we find no traces of Jaques,
Touchstone, Audrey, William, Dennis, Le Beau, Amiens, Sir
Oliver Martext; nothing, indeed, that could yield the slightest hint towards those characters. It scarce need be said
that these superaddings are enough of themselves to transform the play into a new creation, pouring through all its
veins a free and lively circulation of the most original wit
and humor and poetry. And by a judicious indefiniteness
as to persons and places, Shakespeare has greatly idealized
the work, throwing it at a romantic distance and weaving
about it all the witchery of poetical perspective, while the
whole is in such harmony with the laws of the imagination
that the breaches of geographical order are never noticed,
save by such as cannot understand poetry without a map.

No one at all competent to judge in the matter will suppose that Shakespeare could have been really indebted to
Lodge for any of the characters in *As You Like It*. He
merely borrowed certain names and incidents for the bodying
forth of conceptions purely his own. The resemblance is
all in the drapery and circumstances of the representation,
not in the individuals. For instance, we can easily imagine
Rosalind in a hundred scenes not here represented, for
she is a substantive personal being, such as we may detach
and consider apart from the particular order wherein she
stands; but we can discover in her no likeness to Lodge's

heroine, save that of name and situation : take away the similarity here, and there is nothing to indicate any sort of relationship between the heroines of the play and the romance. And it is significant that, though Shakespeare here borrows so freely, there is no sign of any borrowing in the work itself : we can detect no foreign influences, no secondhand touches, nothing to suggest that any part of the thing had ever been thought of before — what he took being so thoroughly assimilated with what he gave that the whole seems to have come fresh from nature and his own mind.

Shakespeare generally preferred to make up his plots and stories out of such materials as were most familiar to his audience. Of this we have many examples, but the fact is too well known to need dwelling upon. Though surpassingly rich in fertility and force of invention, he was notwithstanding singularly economical and sparing in the use of it; which aptly shows how free he was from everything like a sensational spirit or habit of mind. Nature was everything to him, novelty nothing, or next to nothing. The true, not the new, was always the soul of his purpose. Than this nothing could better approve the moral healthiness of his genius; hence, in great part, his noble superiority to the intellectual and literary fashions of his time. He understood these perfectly, but he deliberately rejected them, or rather struck quite above or beyond them. We rarely meet with anything that savors of modishness in his workmanship. Probably the best judgment ever pronounced upon him is Ben Jonson's, " He was not of an age, but for all time." For even so it is with the permanences of our intellectual and imaginative being that he deals, and not with any transiencies of popular or fashionable excitement or pursuit. And as he cared little for the new, so he was all the stronger in that which does not grow old and which lives on from age to age in the perennial, unwithering freshness of truth and nature. To be carried hither and thither by the shifting mental epidemics of the day is but a tacit confession of weakness or disease ; it only proves that one has not strength of mind enough to "feel the soul of nature," or to live at peace with the solidities of reason. And because the attractions of mere novelty had no force with Shakespeare, because his mind dwelt far above the currents of intellectual fashion and convention, his dramas stand " exempt from the wrongs of time " ; and the study of them is a wholesome discipline in those forms and sources of interest which underlie and outlast all the flitting specialties of mode and custom —

> Truths that wake,
> To perish never;
> Which neither listlessness, nor mad endeavour,
> Nor Man nor Boy,
> Nor all that is at enmity with joy,
> Can utterly abolish or destroy !

"ALL THE WORLD'S A STAGE"

The thought in the metaphor with which the famous speech of Jaques, II, vii, 138, begins, seems to be as old and as universal as the art of acting. It is found in the Greek anthology and in Latin literature. Lucian works out the idea elaborately; to Petronius is attributed *Non duco contentionis funem, dum constet inter nos, quod fere totus mundus exerceat histrioniam*,[1] which, in the form, *Totus*

---

[1] " Petronius had not been translated in Shakespeare's time." — Douce.

mundus agit histrionem, is said to have been the motto on
the Globe Theatre, built in 1599 by Richard Burbage and
his brother Cuthbert, where, as Shakespeare himself was one
of the shareholders, it is extremely probable that *As You
Like It* was one of the first plays given. Elizabethan literature abounds in expressions of the same general idea of
this world being but a stage "and all the men and women
merely players." Some of the best known, for example that
of Thomas Heywood in *The Author to His Booke,* or Ben
Jonson's in *The New Inn* (I, i, "When I consider all the
world 's a play"), were written after *As You Like It.* But in
Sidney's *Arcadia* (written probably 1578–1580, first printed
1590) we have, "She found the world but a wearisome stage
to her, where she played a part against her will." So, too, in
Richard Edwardes's 'tragical comedy,' *Damon and Pithias*
(licensed 1566, and first printed apparently in 1571) :

> Pythagoras said, that this world was like a stage,
> Where many play their parts : the lookers on, the sage
> Philosophers are, saith he, whose part is to learn
> The manners of all nations.

Shakespeare himself had already made use of the figure
in *The Merchant of Venice,* I, i, 77–79 :

> I hold the world but as the world, Gratiano,
> A stage where every man must play a part,
> And mine a sad one.

"SEVEN AGES"

Such a division of human life into certain stages or epochs
as Jaques makes, II, vii, 142–165, is found in Greek, Latin,
and later Hebrew literature. In some Greek verses attributed to Solon, the life of man is divided into ten ages of

seven years each. Proclus is said to have made the distribution into seven ages, "over each of which one of the seven planets was supposed to rule. . . . Hippocrates likewise divided the life of man into seven ages, but differs from Proclus in the number of years allotted to each period." — Malone. Fourteen periods are given in the *Mishna*, the body of the 'Oral Law' of the Jews redacted in the third century ; and in the *Midrash*, the Hebrew exposition of the Old Testament made between the sixth and twelfth centuries, the division is into seven periods. A poem upon the ten stages of life was written about the year 1150 by the great Hebrew scholar and exegete Abraham ben Meir ibn Ezra, the Rabbi ben Ezra of Browning's poem. In *Arnold's Chronicle*, a famous fifteenth century miscellany, is a chapter entitled "The vii Ages of Man living in the World." Henley thinks that Shakespeare took his hint for the famous passage from some of the pictorial representations of the theme which were popular in Europe in the fifteenth and sixteenth centuries. But what Shakespeare found neither in old woodcuts nor in mediæval lore are the terse expression, supreme artistry in description, and peculiar Jaques cynicism shown in the emphasis put upon the unlovely aspects of human life in each of the seven ages.

THE TITLE

While, as indicated below under "General Characteristics," the ground idea of the play is indicated by the title *As You Like It*,[1] there is strong probability that the title itself

[1] *Comme il vous plaira* is the title George Sand gave to her French adaptation of the play in which Jaques was made the hero.

was suggested by this passage in Lodge's epistle dedicatory
" To the Gentlemen Readers " :

> Gentlemen, look not here to find anie sprigs of *Pallas* bay tree,
> nor to heare the humour of any amorous Lawreate, nor the pleasing
> vaine of anie eloquent Orator : *Nolo altum sapere*, they be matters
> above my capacitie ; the Coblers checke shall never light on my
> head, *Ne sutor ultra crepidam*, I will go no further than the latchet,
> and then all is well. Heere you may perhaps finde som leaves of
> *Venus* mirtle, but heawen down by a souldier with his curtleaxe,
> not bought with the allurement of a filed tongue. To be briefe
> Gentlemen, roome for a souldier and a sailer, that gives you the
> fruits of his labors that he wrought in the *Ocean*, when everie line
> was wet with a surge, and every humorous passion countercheckt
> with a storme. If you like it, so ; and yet I will be yours in duetie,
> if you bee mine in favour.[1]

Tieck conjectured that the title was a kind of rejoinder
to Ben Jonson's boasting lines with which the epilogue of
Cynthia's Revels closes :

> I 'll only speak what I have heard him say,
> " By —— 't is good, and if you like 't, you may."

Apart from such a rejoinder being most uncharacteristic
of Shakespeare, the date of the production of *Cynthia's
Revels* is fatal to the Tieck theory. On the other hand, it
is quite in keeping with the satire on contemporaries in
Cynthia's Revels to read in these lines of the epilogue a
covert sneer at the title of Shakespeare's play.

---

[1] This is an excellent specimen of Lodge's euphuistic diction.
The orthography is that of the first edition of *Rosalynde*.

II. DATE OF COMPOSITION

EXTERNAL EVIDENCE

1. *The Stationers' Registers.* The earliest reference to
As You Like It is the following entry in *The Stationers'
Registers* :[1]

> my lord chamberlens menns plaies Entred

27 may 1600   viz

to master   A moral of clothe breches and velvet hose
   Robertes

27 May   Allarum to London
To hym

4 Augusti

> As you like yt | a booke
> Henry the Ffift | a booke
> Euery man in his humour | a booke   }to be staied[2]
> The commedie of muche A doo about-nothing
>   a booke |

While *As You Like It* and the three companion plays have
no year attached to the ' 4 August,' there is no question
that the year 1600 is implied. Apart from the proximity
of ' 1600 ' in the previous entry, we find that later in the
same month, with the year 1600 clearly given, *Henry the
Fifth*, *Every Man in His Humour*, and *Much Ado About
Nothing* are entered again, the ' staying ' having been
removed. In the case of *As You Like It*, then, 1600 may
be regarded as a *terminus ante quem* or latest limit to the
time of composition. Why *As You Like It* was not entered
again with the others has led to much conjecture. W. Aldis
Wright is strongly of the opinion that the announcement of

---

[1] Professor E. Arber's *Transcripts of The Stationers' Registers*
(1554–1640), 4 vols., 1875–1877.

[2] ' To be staied ' is the old expression for ' not to be printed.'

its publication was premature : "the play may not have been ready." In support of this he contends that in *As You Like It*, "even in the form in which it has come down to us, there are marks of hasty work which seem to indicate that it was hurriedly finished." [1] There is more probability that the 'staying' was the result of a direct attempt on the part of Shakespeare, or some one acting for him, to prevent the piratical publication of a popular new play, the circulation of which in book form would seriously interfere with its business success and the receipts at the theater. Dr. Furness conjectures that it was the 'bad reputation' of James Roberts (the publisher of the Roberts Quarto of *The Merchant of Venice;* his name is in the margin of the entry in *The Stationers' Registers* given above) "which caused the printing of these plays when first offered to be forbidden."

2. *Palladis Tamia. As You Like It* is not mentioned by Francis Meres in the list of twelve Shakespeare plays given in the *Palladis Tamia*, 1598 ; and as it was likely to be mentioned in that famous list on account of its popular qualities if it had been published, the negative evidence favors the date of composition as being not earlier than 1598.

INTERNAL EVIDENCE

1. *Quotation from Marlowe.* In III, v, 80, 81, we have :

> Dead shepherd, now I find thy saw of might, —
> "Who ever lov'd that lov'd not at first sight?"

The quotation is from Marlowe's *Hero and Leander*, first published in 1598, five years after Marlowe's death. While

[1] Introduction, *As You Like It*, Clarendon Press edition, 1876.

it is possible that this poem may have had a manuscript circulation prior to 1598, it is not likely for two reasons : (1) the poem was unfinished at the time of the author's death, and (2) in contemporary literature there are no quotations from it before 1598, but several after that date.

This bit of internal evidence strengthens the negative external evidence based on the fact that the play is not mentioned in the *Palladis Tamia*.

2. *Time and Place Allusions.* Attempts have been made to base evidence upon Rosalind's references to " pretty oaths that are not dangerous," IV, i, 166, and the " not damnable " art of a magician, V, ii, 57 ; upon the simile " like Diana in the fountain," IV, i, 139 ; upon the allusion to ' half-pence ' in III, ii, 333; upon " east to western Ind," III, ii, 80; and upon " More free from peril than the envious court," II, i, 4 ; but nothing satisfactory has resulted from all the learned investigation and ingenious research involved.

3. *Tests of Diction and Verse Mechanism.* The rigid application of these tests, less available in the case of *As You Like It* because about half the play is in prose, strengthens evidence for the date of composition being between 1598 and 1600.

The cumulative evidence based upon external and internal tests favors 1599–1600 as the date of composition. The only Shakespearian critic of authority who stands for a much later date is Capell (1765), but the evidence of *The Stationers' Registers* was not available to him when he assigned the date of composition to 1607.

III. EDITIONS

The entry in *The Stationers' Registers* given above makes clear that a Quarto edition of *As You Like It* was planned for 1600 — the year that saw the publication of at least ten Shakespeare Quartos; but while hopes have been entertained by Staunton and others that an *As You Like It* Quarto may yet be discovered, such a thing is extremely unlikely, as when Jaggard and Blount received permission to print the First Folio, *As You Like It* is on the list of plays "not formerly entred to other men." It was published for the first time in the First Folio (1623), designated in this edition F_1. It stands between *The Merchant of Venice* and *The Taming of the Shrew*, and runs from page 185 to page 207 inclusive. The printing is excellent, and there is every evidence that the text is sound and trustworthy. The text of the Second Folio, F_2 (1632), the Third Folio, F_3 (1663, 1664), and the Fourth Folio, F_4 (1685), is almost identical with that of the First Folio; the few interesting variations that exist are indicated in the textual notes of this edition.

IV. DRAMATIC STRUCTURE

Shakespeare is always peculiarly happy in what is known technically as the exposition, or introduction, of a play. The first scene of the first act of *As You Like It* is an excellent example of this skill. It tells the audience something of the circumstances of all the leading characters and prepares for every tangle in the complication, or rising action. The climax is in the meeting of Rosalind and Orlando in the forest of Arden in the second scene of the third act. In the resolution, or falling action, is given in delightful balance the progress of the wooing of the four pairs of lovers — Audrey and Touchstone, Phebe and Silvius, Celia and Oliver, in symmetrical subordination and pleasing contrast to the central figures, Rosalind and Orlando. " Now up, now down, as bokets in a welle " — such are the conditions of the wooing and the winning until the happy dénouement of conventional comedy is reached in the dance under the greenwood tree.

V. DICTION AND VERSIFICATION

PROSE

More than half of *As You Like It* is written in prose,[1] probably due to the influence of Sidney's *Arcadia* and Lodge's *Rosalynde* and the general literary fashion in favor of prose pastorals. The prose of *As You Like It* is of two distinct kinds — the prose spoken by Touchstone, Audrey, and William representing the speech of servants and country folks, and the witty sparkling prose of high comedy as in Rosalind's conversations. The former is a development of the humorous prose found, for example, in Greene's comedies that deal with country life ; the latter is a development of Lyly's essentially euphuistic prose. In Shakespeare's hands the two kinds reach new and unexpected developments ; and in this play are passages of such strength and idiomatic excellence as give Shakespeare a supreme place as a master of expression in prose.

[1] According to Furnivall's table, 1681 lines of prose to 925 of blank verse.

Blank Verse

The blank verse of *As You Like It*, while free from the obvious restraint and regularity which mark that of Shakespeare's earlier plays, does not reach the swing and movement of that in the great tragedies and the later comedies. Much of it is normal five-stress iambic verse with a tendency to end-stopped lines, balanced by a goodly proportion of double endings. Here and there in the more impassioned scenes there are adumbrations of the grand style of *Hamlet* and *The Tempest*.

Rhyme

1. *Couplets. As You Like It* shows the marked decrease in the use of rhymed couplets in the dialogue which distinguishes *The Merchant of Venice* and the plays of Shakespeare's maturity from the earlier comedies. Most of the rhymed couplets in *As You Like It* are either tags at the end of scenes or for the purpose of giving edge and distinction to such proverbial wisdom as Adam occasionally indulges in. Orlando's soliloquy in the forest, III, ii, 1–10, is in two quatrains rhyming alternately and closed by a couplet — a Shakespeare sonnet short of a quatrain.

2. *Orlando's Verses.* Like the scrolls within the caskets in *The Merchant of Venice*, Orlando's poem in praise of Rosalind, III, ii, 80–87, is in four-stress trochaic verse catalectic ; so, of course, is Touchstone's 'false gallop.' In the poem Celia reads, III, ii, 117–146, the lines rhyme alternately and close with six normal four-stress iambic lines.

3. *Songs.* The exquisite songs, "Under the greenwood tree," II, v, 1–8 ; "Blow, blow, thou winter wind," II, vii, 173–189 ; "What shall he have that kill'd the deer?" IV,

ii, 10–18, and " It was a lover and his lass," V, iii, 15–32, are in iambic verse with trochaic and amphibrachic effects in the refrains.

VI. THE CHARACTERS

As You Like It is exceedingly rich and varied in character. The several persons stand out round and clear in themselves, yet their distinctive traits in a remarkable degree sink quietly into the feelings without reporting themselves in the understanding ; for which cause the clumsy methods of criticism are little able to give them expression. Subtile indeed must be the analysis that should reproduce them to the intellect without help from dramatic art.

Properly speaking, the play has no hero ; for, though Orlando occupies the foreground, the characters are mainly coördinate ; the design of the work precluding any subordination among them. Diverted by fortune from all their cherished plans and purposes, they pass before us in just that moral and intellectual dishabille which best reveals their indwelling graces of mind and heart. Schlegel remarks that " the poet seems to have aimed, throughout, at showing that nothing is wanting to call forth the poetry that has its dwelling in nature and the human mind, but to throw off all artificial restraint and restore both to their native liberty." This is well said ; but it should be observed that the persons have already been " purified by suffering " ; and that it was under the discipline of social restraint that they developed the virtues which make them go right without such restraint, as indeed they do, while we are conversing with them. Because they have not hitherto been altogether free to do as they would, therefore it is that they are good and beautiful in doing as they have a mind to now. After all, the ordinary conditions of social and domestic life give us far more than they take away. It requires a long schooling in the *prescriptions* of order and rectitude to fit us for being left to ourselves. In some sense indeed it is a great enlargement of liberty to be rid of all the loves and duties and reverences which the past may have woven about us ; and many there are who seem to place freedom of mind in having nothing to look up to, nothing to respect outside of themselves. But human virtue does not grow in this way, and the stream must soon run dry if cut off from the spring. The liberty that goes by unknitting the bands of reverence and dissolving the ties that draw and hold men together in the charities of a common life is not the liberty that Shakespeare teaches. It is true, however, that in *As You Like It* the better transpirations of character are mainly conducted in the eye of nature, where the passions and vanities that so much disfigure human life find little to stir them into act. In the freedom of their woodland resort, and with the native inspirations of the place to kindle and gladden them, the persons have but to live out the handsome thoughts which they have elsewhere acquired. Man's tyranny has indeed driven them into banishment ; but their virtues are much more the growth of the place they are banished from than of the place they are banished to.

ORLANDO

Orlando is altogether such a piece of young manhood as it does one good to be with. He has no special occasion for heroism, yet we feel that there is plenty of heroic stuff in him.

Brave, gentle, modest, and magnanimous; never thinking
of his high birth but to avoid dishonoring it; in his noble-
heartedness forgetting, and causing others to forget, his
nobility of rank, he is every way just such a man as all true
men would choose for their best friend. His persecuting
brother, talking to himself, describes him as " never school'd,
and yet learn'd ; full of noble device ; of all sorts enchantingly belov'd; and indeed so much in the heart of the world,
and especially of my own people, who best know him, that I
am altogether mispris'd " ; and this description is amply
justified by his behavior. The whole intercourse between
him and the faithful old retainer Adam is replete on both
sides with that full-souled generosity in whose eye the nobil-
ities of nature are always sure of recognition.

Shakespeare evidently delighted in a certain natural harmony of character wherein virtue is free and spontaneous,
like the breathing of perfect health. And such is Orlando.
He is therefore good without effort ; nay, it would require
some effort for him to be otherwise ; his soul gravitating
towards goodness as of its own accord : " In his proper
motion he ascends ; descent and fall to him is adverse."
And perhaps the nearest he comes to being aware of his
virtue is when it triumphs over a mighty temptation ; that
is, when he sees his unnatural brother in extreme peril ;

> But kindness, nobler ever than revenge,
> And nature, stronger than his just occasion,

made him risk his own life to save Oliver ; and even in this
case the divine art of overcoming evil with good seems
more an instinct than a conscious purpose with him. This
is one of the many instances wherein Shakespeare delivers

the highest results of Christian discipline as drawing so deeply and so creatively into the heart as to work out with the freedom and felicity of native original impulse.

THE BANISHED DUKE

The banished Duke exemplifies the best sense of nature as thoroughly informed and built up with Christian discipline and religious efficacy; so that the asperities of life do but make his thoughts run the smoother. How sweet, yet how considerative and firm, is everything about his temper and moral frame! He sees all that is seen by the most keen-eyed satirist, yet is never moved to be satirical, because he looks with wiser and therefore kindlier eyes. The enmity of fortune is fairly disarmed by his patience; her shots are all wasted against his breast, garrisoned as it is with the forces of charity and peace: his soul is made storm-proof by gentleness and truth: exile, penury, the ingratitude of men, the malice of the elements, what are they to him? He has the grace to sweeten away their venom, and to smile the sting out of them. He loves to stay himself upon the compensations of life, and to feed his gentler affections by dwelling upon the good which adversity opens to him, or the evil from which it withdraws him; and so he rejoices in finding " these woods more free from peril than the envious court." In his philosophy, so bland, benignant, and contemplative, the mind tastes the very luxury of rest and has an antepast of measureless content.

TOUCHSTONE

Touchstone, though he nowhere strikes so deep a chord
within us as the poor fool in *King Lear*, is, I think, the most
entertaining of Shakespeare's privileged characters. And he
is indeed a mighty delectable fellow ; wise, too, and full of the
most insinuative counsel. How choicely does his grave, acute
nonsense moralize the scenes wherein he moves ! Professed
clown though he be, and as such ever hammering away with
artful awkwardness at a jest, a strange kind of humorous
respect still waits upon him notwithstanding. It is curious
to observe how Shakespeare takes care to let us know, from
the first, that beneath the affectations of his calling some
precious sentiments have been kept alive ; that far within
the fool there is laid up a secret reserve of the man, ready
to leap forth and combine with better influences as soon as
the incrustations of art are thawed and broken up. This is
partly done in the scene where Rosalind and Celia arrange
for their flight from the usurper's court. Rosalind proposes,

> But, cousin, what if we assay'd to steal
> The clownish fool out of your father's court ?
> Would he not be a comfort to our travel ?

And Celia replies,

> He 'll go along o'er the wide world with me ;
> Leave me alone to woo him.

Where we learn that some remnants, at least, of a manly
heart in him have asserted their force in the shape of unself-
ish regards, strong as life, for whatever is purest and loveliest
in the characters about him. He would rather starve or
freeze, with Celia near him, than feed high and lie warm

where his eye cannot find her. If, with this fact in view, our honest esteem does not go out towards him, then we, I think, are fools in a worse sense than he is.

So much for the substantial manhood of Touchstone, and for Shakespeare's human-heartedness in thus putting us in communication with it. As for the other points of his character, it is impossible to draw a reader into them by any turn of analysis. Used to a life cut off from human sympathies; stripped of the common responsibilities of the social state; living for no end but to make aristocratic idlers laugh; one therefore whom nobody heeds enough to resent or be angry at anything he says; —of course his habit is to speak all for effect, nothing for truth: instead of reflecting the natural force and image of things, his vocation is to wrest and trans-shape them from their true form and pressure. Thus a strange wilfulness and whimsicality has wrought itself into the substance of his mind. He takes nothing for what it is in itself, but only for the odd quirks of thought he can twist out of it. Yet his nature is not so "subdued to what it works in" but that, amidst the scenes and inspirations of the forest, the fool quickly slides into the man; the supervenings of the place so running into and athwart what he brings with him that his character comes to be as dappled and motley as his dress. Even the new passion which there overtakes him has a touch of his wilfulness in it: when he falls in love, as he really does, nothing seems to inspire and draw him more than the unattractiveness of the object, thus approving that even so much of nature as survives in him is not content to run in natural channels.

JAQUES

Jaques is a universal favorite, as indeed he well may be, for he is certainly one of Shakespeare's happiest conceptions. Without being at all unnatural, he has an amazing fund of peculiarity. Enraptured out of his senses at the voice of a song ; thrown into a paroxysm of laughter at sight of the motley-clad and motley-witted fool ; and shedding the twilight of his merry-sad spirit over all the darker spots of human life and character, he represents the abstract and sum total of an utterly useless yet perfectly harmless man, seeking wisdom by abjuring its first principle. An odd choice mixture of reality and affectation, he does nothing but think, yet avowedly thinks to no purpose ; or rather thinking is with him its own end. On the whole, if in Touchstone there is much of the philosopher in the fool, in Jaques there is not less of the fool in the philosopher; so that the German critic, Ulrici, is not so wide of the mark in calling them " two fools."

Jaques is equally wilful, too, with Touchstone, in his turn of thought and speech, though not so conscious of it ; and as he plays his part more to please himself, so he is propor- tionably less open to the healing and renovating influences of nature. We cannot justly affirm, indeed, that " the soft blue sky did never melt into his heart," as Wordsworth says of his Peter Bell ; but he shows more of resistance than all the other persons to the poetries and eloquences of the place. Tears are a great luxury to him : he sips the cup of woe with all the gust of an epicure. Still his temper is by no means sour : fond of solitude, he is nevertheless far from being unsocial. The society of good men, provided they be in adversity, has great charms for him. He likes to be with those who, though deserving the best, still have the worst: virtue wronged, buffeted, oppressed, is his special delight, because such moral discrepancies offer the most salient points to his cherished meditations. [He himself enumerates nearly all the forms of melancholy except his own, which I take to be the melancholy of self-love.] And its effect in his case is not unlike that of Touchstone's art; inasmuch as he greatly delights to see things otherwise than as they really are, and to make them speak out some meaning that is not in them; that is, their plain and obvious sense is not to his taste. Nevertheless his melancholy is grateful, because free from any dash of malignity. His morbid habit of mind seems to spring from an excess of generative virtue. And how racy and original is everything that comes from him ! as if it bubbled up from the center of his being; while his perennial fullness of matter makes his company always delightful. The Duke loves especially to meet him in his 'sullen fits,' because he then overflows with his most idiomatic humor. After all, the worst that can be said of Jaques is that the presence of men who are at once fortunate and deserving corks him up; which may be only another way of saying that he cannot open out and run over, save where things are going wrong.

ROSALIND AND CELIA

It is something uncertain whether Jaques or Rosalind be the greater attraction: there is enough in either to make the play a continual feast, though her charms are less liable to be staled by use, because they result from health of mind and symmetry of character, so that in her presence the head and the heart draw together perfectly. She never starts any moral or emotional reluctances in our converse with her : all our sympathies go along with her freely, because she never jars upon them, or touches them against the grain.

For wit, this strange, queer, lovely being is fully equal to Beatrice, yet nowise resembling her. A soft, subtile, nimble essence, consisting in one knows not what, and springing up one can hardly tell how, her wit neither stings nor burns, but plays briskly and airily over all things within its reach, enriching and adorning them ; insomuch that one could ask no greater pleasure than to be the continual theme of it. In its irrepressible vivacity it waits not for occasion, but runs on forever, and we wish it to run on forever. We have a sort of faith that her dreams are made up of cunning, quirkish, graceful fancies, her wits being in a frolic even when she is asleep. And her heart seems a perennial spring of affectionate cheerfulness : no trial can break, no sorrow chill, her flow of spirits ; even her sighs are breathed forth in a wrappage of innocent mirth ; an arch, roguish smile irradiates her saddest tears. No sort of unhappiness can live in her company : it is a joy even to stand her chiding ; for, faster than her tongue doth make offense, her eye doth heal it up.

So much for her choice idiom of wit. She also aptly illustrates Shakespeare's peculiar use of humor. The difference of wit and humor is too well understood to need any special exposition. But the two often go together ; though there is a form of wit, much more common, that burns and dries the juices all out of the mind, and turns it into a kind of sharp, stinging wire. Now Rosalind's sweet establishment is thoroughly saturated with humor, and this too of the freshest and wholesomest quality. And the effect of her humor is, as it were, to lubricate all her faculties, and make her thoughts run brisk and glib even when grief has possession of her heart. Through this interfusive power, her organs of play are held in perfect concert with her springs of serious thought. Hence she is outwardly merry and inwardly sad at the same time. We may justly say that she laughs out her sadness, or plays out her seriousness : the sorrow that is swelling her breast puts her wits and spirits into a frolic ; and in the mirth that overflows through her tongue we have a relish of the grief with which her heart is charged. And our sympathy with her inward state is the more divinely moved, forasmuch as she thus, with inde-scribable delicacy, touches it through a masquerade of play-fulness. Yet, beneath all her frolicsomeness, we feel that there is a firm basis of thought and womanly dignity ; so that she never laughs away our respect.

[It is quite remarkable how, in respect of her disguise, Rosalind just reverses the conduct of Viola, yet with much the same effect. For, though she seems as much at home in her male attire as if she had always worn it, this never strikes us otherwise than as an exercise of skill for the per-fecting of her masquerade. And on the same principle her occasional freedoms of speech serve to deepen our sense of her innate delicacy ; they being manifestly intended as a part of her disguise, and springing from the feeling that it is far less indelicate to go a little out of her character, in order to prevent any suspicion of her sex, than it would be to hazard such a suspicion by keeping strictly within her character. In other words, her free talk bears much the same relation to her character as her dress does to her per-son, and is therefore becoming to her even on the score of feminine modesty.] Celia appears well worthy of a place

beside her whose love she shares and repays. Instinct with
the soul of moral beauty and female tenderness, the friendship of these more than sisters " mounts to the seat of grace
within the mind."

> We still have slept together,
> Rose at an instant, learn'd, play'd, eat together;
> And wheresoe'er we went, like Juno's swans,
> Still we went coupled and inseparable.

VII. GENERAL CHARACTERISTICS

The general drift and temper, or, as some of the German
critics would say, the ground idea of this play, is aptly
hinted by the title. As for the beginnings of what is here
represented, these do not greatly concern us ; most of them
lie back out of our view, and the rest are soon lost sight of
in what grows out of them ; but the issues, of which there
are many, are all exactly to our mind ; we feel them to be
just about right, and would not have them otherwise. For
example, touching Frederick and Oliver, our wish is that
they should repent, and repair the wrong they have done,
in brief that they should become good ; which is precisely
what takes place ; and as soon as they do this, they naturally love those who were good before. Jaques, too, is so
fitted to moralize the discrepancies of human life, so happy
and at home and withal so agreeable in that exercise, that
we would not he should follow the good Duke when in his
case those discrepancies are composed. The same might
easily be shown in respect of the other issues. Indeed any
genial, considerate reader might be asked, Does not everything turn out just *as you like it?* Moreover there is an

indefinable something about the play that puts us in a receptive frame of mind; that opens the heart, soothes away all querulousness and fault-finding, and makes us easy and apt to be pleased. Thus Shakespeare here disposes us to like things as they come, and at the same time takes care that they shall come as we like. The whole play, indeed, is *as you like it*.

Much has been said by one critic and another about the improbabilities in this play. To such the best reply is the criticism of the poet Campbell: "Before I say more of this dramatic treasure, I must absolve myself by a confession as to some of its improbabilities. Rosalind asks her cousin Celia, 'Whither shall we go?' and Celia answers, 'To seek my uncle in the forest of Arden.' But, arrived there, and having purchased a cottage and sheep farm, neither the daughter nor niece of the banished Duke seem to trouble themselves much to inquire about either father or uncle. The lively and natural-hearted Rosalind discovers no impatience to embrace her sire, until she has finished her masked courtship with Orlando. But Rosalind was in love, as I have been with the comedy these forty years; and love is blind; for until a late period my eyes were never couched so as to see this objection. The truth however is, that love is wilfully blind: and now that my eyes are opened, I shut them against the fault. Away with your best-proved improbabilities, when the heart has been touched and the fancy fascinated."

Again; the bringing of lions, serpents, palm trees, rustic shepherds, and banished noblemen together in the forest of Arden is a strange piece of geographical license, which certain critics have not failed to make merry with. Perhaps they did not see that the very grossness of the thing proves it to have been designed. Shakespeare keeps his geography true enough whenever he has cause to do so. He knew, at all events, that lions did not roam at large in France. By this irregular combination of actual things, he informs the whole with ideal effect, giving to this charming issue of his brain "a local habitation and a name," that it may link in with our flesh-and-blood sympathies, and at the same time turning it into a wild, wonderful, remote, fairy-land region, where all sorts of poetical things may take place without the slightest difficulty. Of course Shake-speare would not have done thus, but that he saw quite through the grand critical humbug which makes the proper effect of a work of art depend upon our belief in the actual occurrence of the thing represented. But your "critic grave and cool" is one who, like Wordsworth's "model of a child,"

> Can string you names of districts, cities, towns,
> The whole world over, tight as beads of dew
> Upon a gossamer thread : he sifts, he weighs ;
> All things are put to question ; he must live
> Knowing that he grows wiser every day,
> Or else not live at all, and seeing too
> Each little drop of wisdom as it falls
> Into the dimpling cistern of his heart.
> O, give us once again the wishing-cap
> Of Fortunatus, and the invisible coat
> Of Jack the Giant-killer, Robin Hood,
> And Sabra in the forest with Saint George !
> The child, whose love is here, at least doth reap
> One precious gain, that he forgets himself.

The whole of *As You Like It* is replete with a beauty so delicate yet so intense that we feel it everywhere, but can never tell especially where it is or in what it consists. For instance, the descriptions of forest scenery come along so unsought and in such easy, quiet, natural touches that we take in the impression without once noticing what it is that impresses us. Thus there is a certain woodland freshness, a glad, free naturalness, that creeps and steals into the heart before we know it. And the spirit of the place is upon its inhabitants, its genius within them : we almost breathe with them the fragrance of the forest, and listen to " the melodies of woods and winds and waters," and feel

> The power, the beauty, and the majesty,
> That have their haunts in dale, or piny mountain,
> Or forest by slow stream, or pebbly spring.

Even the court fool, notwithstanding all the crystallizing process that has passed upon him, undergoes, as we have seen, a sort of rejuvenescence of his inner man, so that his wit catches at every turn the fresh hues and odors of his new whereabout. Surely Milton had a special eye to this play in the lines :

> And sweetest Shakespeare, Fancy's child,
> Warbles his native wood-notes wild.

Such is *As You Like It.* The play abounds in wild frolicsome graces which cannot be described ; which can only be seen and felt ; and which the hoarse voice of criticism seems to scare away, as the crowing of cocks is said to have scared away the fairy spirits from their nocturnal pastimes. To all which add that the kindlier sentiments everywhere in the play seem playing out in a sort of jubilee. Untied from set purposes and definite aims, the persons come forth with their hearts already tuned, and all

they say and do is music. Envy, jealousy, avarice, revenge,
all the passions that afflict and degrade society, they have
left in the city behind them. And they have brought the
intelligence and refinement of the court without its vanities
and vexations, so that the graces of art and the simplicities
of nature meet together in joyous, loving sisterhood. A
serene and mellow atmosphere of thought encircles and
pervades the actors in this drama, as if on purpose to
illustrate how

> One impulse from a vernal wood
>   May teach you more of man,
> Of moral evil, and of good,
>   Than all the sages can.

Nature throws her protecting arms around them; beauty
pitches her tents before them; heaven rains its riches upon
them; with "no enemy but winter and rough weather,"
peace hath taken up her abode with them; and they have
nothing to do but to "fleet the time carelessly, as they did
in the golden world."

ABBREVIATIONS USED IN THE NOTES

F_1 = First Folio, 1623.

F_2 = Second Folio, 1632.

F_3 = Third Folio, 1664.

F_4 = Fourth Folio, 1685.

Ff = all the seventeenth century Folios.

Rowe = Rowe's editions, 1709, 1714.

Pope = Pope's editions, 1723, 1728.

Theobald = Theobald's editions, 1733, 1740.

Hanmer = Hanmer's edition, 1744.

Johnson = Johnson's edition, 1765.

Capell = Capell's edition, 1768.

Malone = Malone's edition, 1790.

Camb = Cambridge edition (W. A. Wright), 1891.

Clar = Clarendon Press edition (W. A. Wright), 1876.

Furness = H. H. Furness's *A New Variorum. As You Like It*, 1890.

Abbott = E. A. Abbott's *A Shakespearian Grammar*.

Cotgrave = Cotgrave's *Dictionarie of the French and English Tongues*, 1611.

Schmidt = Schmidt's *Shakespeare Lexicon*.

Skeat = Skeat's *An Etymological Dictionary*.

Murray = *A New English Dictionary* (*The Oxford Dictionary*).

Century = *The Century Dictionary*.

Other abbreviations are either self-explanatory or such as are in common use.

CHRONOLOGICAL CHART

Except in the case of Shakespeare's plays (see note) the literature dates refer to first publication

YEAR	SHAKESPEARE BIOGRAPHY: POEMS	SHAKESPEARE PLAYS	BRITISH AND FOREIGN LITERATURE	HISTORY AND BIOGRAPHY
1564	Birth. Baptism, April 26, Stratford-on-Avon		Quart livre de Pantagruel	Michelangelo died. Calvin died. Marlowe born. Galileo born
1565	Father became alderman		Sackville and Norton's Gorboduc printed	Philip II of Spain gave his name to Philippine Islands
1566	Brother Gilbert born		Udall's Roister Doister printed?	Murder of Rizzio
1568	Father, as bailiff of Stratford, entertained Queen's and Earl of Worcester's actors	**NOTE.** The plays in the columns below are arranged in the probable, though purely conjectural, order of composition. Dates appended to plays are those of first publication. Where no date is given, the play was first published in the First Folio (1623). M signifies that the play was mentioned by Meres in the **Palladis Tamia (1598)**	The Bishops' Bible. La Taille's Saülle Furieux. R. Grafton's Chronicle	Mary of Scots a prisoner in England. Ascham died. Coverdale died. Netherlands War of Liberation
1572			Camoens' Os Lusiadas (The Lusiads)	Knox died. Massacre of St. Bartholomew
1573			Tasso's Aminta	Ben Jonson born? Donne born
1574	Brother Richard born		Mirror for Magistrates (third edition)	Earl of Leicester's players licensed
1575			Gammer Gurton's Needle. Golding's Ovid (complete)	Queen Elizabeth at Kenilworth. Palissy lectured on Natural History
1576			The Paradise of Dainty Devices. Gascoigne's Steel Glass	"The Theatre" opened in Finsbury Fields, London, followed by "The Curtain." Hans Sachs died
1577	Father in financial difficulties		Holinshed's Chronicle	Drake sailed to circumnavigate globe

	Shakespeare's Life	Comedies	Histories	Tragedies		
1579	Sister Ann died (aged eight)				Gosson's School of Abuse. North's Plutarch. Lyly's Euphues (pt. 1). Spenser's Shepherd's Calendar	Union of Utrecht. Tasso put in confinement at Ferrara
1580	Brother Edmund born				Montaigne's Essais (first edition)	Brown founded Separatists. Camoens died
1581					Tasso's Gerusalemme Liberata	Dutch Declaration of Independence
1582	Married Anne Hathaway				The Rheims New Testament	Accademia della Crusca founded
1583	Daughter Susanna born				Garnier's Les Juives	Sir Humphrey Gilbert drowned
1584					Lyly's Campaspe. Peele's Arraignment of Paris	William the Silent assassinated. Ivan the Terrible died
1585	Twin children (Hamnet, Judith) born				Guarini's Pastor Fido (1590)	Ronsard died
1586	Probably went to London				Camden's Britannia	Sir Philip Sidney killed
1587					Hakluyt's Four Voyages. Faustbuch (Spiess, Frankfort)	Execution of Mary of Scots
1588					Martin Marprelate: The Epistle	Defeat of Spanish Armada
1589					Puttenham's Art of English Poesie	Henry of Navarre, King of France. Palissy died in Bastille
1590		Love's Labour's Lost (M, 1598)			Marlowe's Tamburlaine. Spenser's Faerie Queene, I-III. Lodge's Rosalynde. Sidney's Arcadia	Battle of Ivry
1591		Comedy of Errors (M)	1 Henry VI / 2 Henry VI		Sidney's Astrophel and Stella. Harington's tr. of Orlando Furioso	Herrick born

CHRONOLOGICAL CHART (CONTINUED)

YEAR	BIOGRAPHY: POEMS	SHAKESPEARE — PLAYS (see note above)			BRITISH AND FOREIGN LITERATURE	HISTORY AND BIOGRAPHY
1592	Greene's attack in Groatsworth of Wit	Two Gentlemen of Verona (M)	Richard III (M, 1597). 3 Henry VI	Romeo and Juliet (M, 1597)	Daniel's Delia. Lyly's Gallathea (Galatea)	Greene died. Montaigne died. London theatres closed through plague
1593	Venus and Adonis (seven editions, 1593-1602)		King John (M). Richard II (M, 1597)	Titus Andronicus (M, 1594)	Peele's Edward I. Barnes's Sonnets	Marlowe died. Herbert born
1594	Lucrece (five editions, 1594-1616)	A Midsummer Night's Dream (M, 1600)			Rinuccini's Dafne. Satire Ménipée	Palestrina ("Princeps Musicæ") died
1595	Valuable contemporary references to Shakespeare	All's Well that Ends Well. Taming of the Shrew			Peele's Old Wives' Tale. Spenser's Epithalamion	Tasso died. Sir Walter Raleigh's expedition to Guiana. Sir J. Hawkins died
1596	Son Hamnet died. Family applied for coat-of-arms	1 Henry IV (M, 1598). 2 Henry IV (M, 1600)			Drayton's Mortimeriados. Faerie Queene, Books IV-VI	Burbage built Blackfriar's Theatre. Descartes born. Sir F. Drake died
1597	Purchased New Place, Stratford	Merry Wives of Windsor, Merchant of Venice (M, 1600)	Henry V (1600)		Bacon's Essays (first edition). Hall's Virgidemiarum	The Tyrone rebellion
1598	Shakespeare acted in Jonson's Every Man in His Humour	Much Ado About Nothing (1600)			Meres's Palladis Tamia. Chapman's Homer (pt. i). Lope de Vega's Arcadia	Peele died. Edict of Nantes
1599	Part proprietor of Globe Theatre, Coat-of-arms granted. The Passionate Pilgrim	As You Like It			Aleman's Guzman de Alfarache. Peele's David and Bethsabe	Spenser died. Globe Theatre built. Oliver Cromwell born
1600	Won a London lawsuit	Twelfth Night			England's Helicon	Calderon born. Bruno died

Year	Shakespeare's life		Plays	Plays	Other literature	Contemporary events
1601	Father died. The Phœnix and Turtle		Julius Cæsar		Jonson's Poetaster	The Essex plot. Rivalry between London adult and boy actors
1602	Purchased more Stratford real estate		Hamlet (1603)		Dekker's Satiro-mastix	Bodleian Library founded
1603	His company acted before the Queen			Troilus and Cressida (1609)	Jonson's Sejanus	Queen Elizabeth died. Millenary Petition
1604	Sued Rogers at Stratford		Othello	Measure for Measure	Marlowe's Faustus (1588-1589)	Hampton Court Conference
1605	Godfather to William D'Avenant		Macbeth		Don Quixote (pt. 1)	Gunpowder plot. Sir Thomas Browne born
1606	King Lear given before Court		King Lear (1608)		Chapman's Monsieur D'Olive	Lyly died. Corneille born
1607	Daughter Susanna married Dr. Hall		Timon of Athens		Dekker and Webster's Westward Ho!	Settlement of Jamestown
1608	Birth of granddaughter, Elizabeth Hall. Death of mother (Mary Arden)		Antony and Cleopatra	Pericles (1609)	Captain John Smith's A True Relation. Middleton's A Mad World	Milton born. Quebec founded
1609	Sonnets. A Lover's Complaint		Coriolanus		The Douai Old Testament	Separatists (Pilgrims) in Leyden
1610	Purchased more real estate			Cymbeline	Strachey's Wracke and Redemption	Henry IV (Navarre) assassinated
1611	Subscribed for better highways			Winter's Tale / The Tempest	King James Bible (A.V.). Bellarmine's Puissance du Pape	Gustavus Adolphus, King of Sweden
1613	Invested in London house property. Brother Richard died	Henry VIII			Drayton's Polyolbion	Globe Theatre burned
1616	Made his will. Daughter Judith married Thomas Quiney. Died April 23 (May 3, New Style)				Captain John Smith's New England. Folio edition of Jonson's Poems. D'Aubigné's Les Tragiques (1577)	Cervantes died. Beaumont died. Baffin explores Baffin's Bay. Harvey lectured on the circulation of the blood

AS YOU LIKE IT

DRAMATIS PERSONÆ[1]

DUKE, living in banishment.

FREDERICK, his brother, and usurper of his dominions.

AMIENS, } lords attending on the banished Duke.
JAQUES,[2] }

LE BEAU,[3] a courtier attending upon Frederick.

CHARLES, wrestler to Frederick.

OLIVER, }
JAQUES, } sons of Sir Rowland de Boys.
ORLANDO, }

ADAM, } servants to Oliver.
DENNIS, }

TOUCHSTONE, a clown.

SIR[4] OLIVER MARTEXT, a vicar.

CORIN, } shepherds.
SILVIUS,[5] }

WILLIAM, a country fellow, in love with Audrey.

A person representing Hymen.

ROSALIND, daughter to the banished Duke.

CELIA, daughter to Frederick.

PHEBE, a shepherdess.

AUDREY,[6] a country wench.

Lords, Pages, Foresters, and other Attendants.

SCENE: *Oliver's house, Duke Frederick's court, and the Forest of Arden.*

[1] DRAMATIS PERSONÆ. First given by Rowe (1709). After the names Corin and Sylvius (Silvius), Rowe (1714) added 'A clown in love with Audrey,' and 'William, another clown in love with Audrey.' Capell added to Rowe's list 'a person representing Hymen.'

[2] JAQUES. In certain districts of England this name is and has been pronounced as a monosyllable, but Shakespeare, Kyd, Greene, and Beaumont and Fletcher treat it as a dissyllable, and, wherever the name occurs in their verse, the metre requires it to be pronounced so. See Furness.

[3] LE BEAU. This name is spelled 'Le Beu' everywhere in the First Folio, except in the stage direction upon the courtier's first entrance, where it is given as in the text.

[4] SIR. See note, p. 90, l. 36.

[5] SILVIUS. So the name is spelled in the First Folio. Rowe adopted 'Sylvius.'

[6] AUDREY. See note, p. 87.

2

ACT I

Scene I. *Orchard of* Oliver's *house*

Enter Orlando *and* Adam

Orlando. As I remember, Adam, it was upon this fashion bequeath'd me by will but poor a thousand crowns ; and, as thou say'st, charg'd my brother, on his blessing, to breed me well : and there begins my sadness. My brother Jaques he keeps at school, and report speaks goldenly of

Orchard of Oliver's *house* not in Ff. | An Orchard Rowe | Oliver's House Pope | Oliver's Orchard Theobald.

2. **fashion bequeath'd** Ff | fashion : bequeathed Camb. — **poor a** F₁ | a poor F₂F₃F₄ Rowe.

Scene I. The division into scenes in this edition is that given in the First Folio. The division adopted by Pope, and followed by some editors, will be indicated in the textual notes.

Adam. There is an interesting tradition quoted by Steevens as found in "the manuscript papers of the late Mr. Oldys," that Shakespeare himself took the part of Adam.

2. In previous editions of Hudson's Shakespeare, the reading 'fashion, — he bequeathed,' first suggested, though with different punctuation, by Sir William Blackstone and also by Ritson, was adopted. But while there is abundant reason for the pause after 'fashion,' the insertion of 'he' is unnecessary. The ellipsis of the nominative is a not unusual Shakespearian construction (Abbott, § 399), and here the omission of 'he' (i.e. 'my father'; cf. Orlando's speech, "My father charged you in his will," etc.) may be intended to show the colloquial eagerness of Orlando's talk with Adam. See Furness. — **poor a thousand.** For a discussion of such transposition, see Abbott, §§ 85, 422.

3. **on** : as the condition of obtaining.

5. **school** : university. So in *Hamlet*, I, ii, 113.

his profit; for my part, he keeps me rustically at home, or, to speak more properly, stays me here at home unkept; for call you that keeping for a gentleman of my birth, that differs not from the stalling of an ox? His horses are bred better; for, besides that they are fair with their feeding, they are taught their manage, and to that end riders dearly hir'd : but I, his brother, gain nothing under him but growth; for the which his animals on his dunghills are as much bound to him as I. Besides this nothing that he so plentifully gives me, the something that nature gave me his countenance seems to take from me : he lets me feed with his hinds, bars me the place of a brother, and, as much as in him lies, mines my gentility with my education. This is it, Adam, that grieves me ; and the spirit of my father, which I think is within me, begins to mutiny against this servitude : I will no longer endure it, though yet I know no wise remedy how to avoid it.   22

ADAM. Yonder comes my master, your brother.

ORLANDO. Go apart, Adam, and thou shalt hear how he will shake me up.   [ADAM *retires*]

22. Here Ff have 'Enter Oliver.'   23. Scene II Pope.

11. **manage** : horse-training. So in *1 Henry IV*, II, iii, 52.

16. **countenance** : treatment. This use of the word is well explained in Selden's *Table-talk : "* The old law was, that when a man was fined, he was to be fined *salvo contenemento*, so as his countenance might be safe ; taking ' countenance ' in the same sense as your countryman does when he says, If you will come unto my house, I will show you the best countenance I can ; that is, not the best face, but the best entertainment."

17. **hinds** : servants. The word in this sense is still in common use in Scotland.

18. What an honorable parentage has done for me he strives to undo by base breeding. — **mines** : undermines. — **gentility** : noble birth.

Enter OLIVER

OLIVER. Now, sir ! what make you here?　　　26

ORLANDO. Nothing : I am not taught to make any thing.

OLIVER. What mar you then, sir?

ORLANDO. Marry, sir, I am helping you to mar that which
God made, a poor unworthy brother of yours, with idleness.

OLIVER. Marry, sir, be better employ'd, and be naught
awhile.　　　32

ORLANDO. Shall I keep your hogs, and eat husks with
them? What prodigal portion have I spent, that I should
come to such penury?　　　35

OLIVER. Know you where you are, sir?

ORLANDO. O, sir, very well : here in your orchard.

OLIVER. Know you before whom, sir?　　　38

ORLANDO. Ay, better than him I am before knows me.
I know you are my eldest brother ; and, in the gentle condition of blood, you should so know me. The courtesy of

26. **what make you** : what are you doing? Orlando plays on the
word 'make' in the sense of 'produce.'

29. **Marry,** which here keeps up the word-play, was frequently
used in colloquial language as a petty oath or intensive ; something
like the Latin *hercle* and *edepol*. This use of 'marry' sprang from a
custom of swearing by St. Mary the Virgin.

31-32. **be naught awhile.** 'Be naught,' or 'go and be naught,'
was formerly a petty execration between anger and contempt, which
has been supplanted by others, as 'be hanged,' 'be cursed,' etc. ;
'awhile,' or 'the while,' was added merely to round the phrase.

34. **prodigal.** Here used proleptically. Shakespeare makes many
allusions to the parable of the Prodigal Son. In previous editions
of Hudson's Shakespeare, Seymour's emendation, " What prodigal's
portion," was adopted.

40-41. **in the gentle condition of blood** : as becomes brothers of
gentle birth and breeding.

nations allows you my better, in that you are the first-born ;
but the same tradition takes not away my blood, were there
twenty brothers betwixt us : I have as much of my father
in me as you ; albeit, I confess, your coming before me is
nearer to his reverence.   46

OLIVER. What, boy !

ORLANDO. Come, come, elder brother, you are too
young in this.

OLIVER. Wilt thou lay hands on me, villain?   50

ORLANDO. I am no villain ; I am the youngest son of
Sir Rowland de Boys ; he was my father ; and he is thrice
a villain that says such a father begot villains. Wert thou
not my brother, I would not take this hand from thy throat
till this other had pull'd out thy tongue for saying so : thou
hast rail'd on thyself.   56

ADAM. Sweet masters, be patient: for your father's remem-
brance, be at accord.

OLIVER. Let me go, I say.   59

ORLANDO. I will not, till I please : you shall hear me.
My father charg'd you in his will to give me good education : you have train'd me like a peasant, obscuring and

52. Boys F1 | Boyes F2F3F4.   57. masters F1 | master F2F3F4.

46. Nearer to him in the right of that reverence which was his due.
47. " The word 'boy' naturally provokes and awakens in Orlando
the sense of his manly powers; and with the retort of 'elder' brother,
he grasps him with firm hands, and makes him feel he is no boy."
— Coleridge. So in Lodge's story: " Though I am eldest by birth,
yet, never having attempted any deedes of Armes, I am yongest to
performe any martial exploytes."
50. villain. As Johnson suggested, while Oliver uses the word
in its modern sense of 'scoundrel,' Orlando probably takes it in its
original meaning of 'one lowborn.'

hiding from me all gentleman-like qualities. The spirit of
my father grows strong in me, and I will no longer endure
it : therefore allow me such exercises as may become a
gentleman, or give me the poor allottery my father left me
by testament; with that I will go buy my fortunes.   67

OLIVER. And what wilt thou do? beg, when that is spent?
Well, sir, get you in : I will not long be troubled with you;
you shall have some part of your will : I pray you, leave me.

ORLANDO. I will no further offend you than becomes
me for my good.   ·   72

OLIVER. Get you with him, you old dog !

ADAM. Is ' old dog ' my reward? Most true, I have lost
my teeth in your service. — God be with my old master !
he would not have spoke such a word.   76

                       [*Exeunt* ORLANDO *and* ADAM]

OLIVER. Is it even so ? begin you to grow upon me? I
will physic your rankness, and yet give no thousand crowns
neither. — Holla, Dennis !   79

                   Enter DENNIS

DENNIS. Calls your worship?

OLIVER. Was not Charles, the Duke's wrestler, here to
speak with me?   82

---

77. Scene III Pope.   larly elsewhere Ff read 'wrastling,'
81. wrestler | wrastler F1 (simi-   'wrastle,' 'wrastled').

63. qualities : occupations, pursuits. Thus the word accords with
' exercises ' in l. 65. Cf. *The Two Gentlemen of Verona*, IV, i, 58 :

          a man of such perfection,
   As we do in our quality much want.

66. allottery: allotted share. Occurs nowhere else in Shakespeare.

78. physic your rankness : heal your overgrowth. Oliver's thought
is that Orlando is growing too big for his station, and so needs to be
taken down. Shakespeare repeatedly uses 'to physic' for 'to heal.'

DENNIS. So please you, he is here at the door, and importunes access to you.

OLIVER. Call him in. [*Exit* DENNIS] 'T will be a good way ; and to-morrow the wrestling is.   86

Enter CHARLES

CHARLES. Good morrow to your worship.

OLIVER. Good Monsieur Charles, what 's the new news at the new court?   89

CHARLES. There 's no news at the court, sir, but the old news : that is, the old Duke is banish'd by his younger brother the new Duke ; and three or four loving lords have put themselves into voluntary exile with him, whose lands and revenues enrich the new Duke; therefore he gives them good leave to wander.   95

OLIVER. Can you tell if Rosalind, the Duke's daughter, be banish'd with her father?   97

CHARLES. O, no ; for the Duke's daughter, her cousin, so loves her, being ever from their cradles bred together, that she would have follow'd her exile, or have died to stay

93. into F_1F_2 | into a F_3F_4.
96. the Duke's | the old Duke's Hanmer.

98. the Duke's | the new Duke's Hanmer.
100. she F_3F_4 | hee F_1 | he F_2.

88. **Good Monsieur Charles.** In previous editions of Hudson's Shakespeare Walker's conjectural 'morrow' was inserted before 'Monsieur,' but the expression in the text is a common salutation.

90. Lettsom suggested the insertion of 'new' before 'court,' and this reading was adopted in previous editions of Hudson's Shakespeare ; as also were the Hanmer emendations in ll. 96, 98.

100. **to stay.** This is an instance of the infinitive used gerundively, or like the Latin gerund, and so the expression is equivalent to 'by staying' or 'from staying.' The usage is frequent in Shakespeare, and sometimes makes his meaning obscure. See Abbott, § 356.

behind her. She is at the court, and no less belov'd of her
uncle than his own daughter; and never two ladies lov'd
as they do.

OLIVER. Where will the old Duke live?   104

CHARLES. They say he is already in the forest of Arden,
and a many merry men with him; and there they live like
the old Robin Hood of England: they say, many young
gentlemen flock to him every day, and fleet the time carelessly, as they did in the golden world.   109

OLIVER. What, you wrestle to-morrow before the new Duke?

105. forest of Arden. While Shakespeare took the name 'Arden'
from Lodge, who undoubtedly meant the forest of Ardennes in
French Flanders, it is an interesting fact that there was a forest of
Arden in Warwickshire, referred to twice by Drayton as the haunt
of nightingales. Arden, too, is the family name of Shakespeare's
mother.

106. a many. See Abbott, § 87. Cf. *Henry V*, IV, i, 127.

107. old Robin Hood. This prince of outlaws and "most gentle
theefe" had his chief residence, according to popular song and
story, in Sherwood Forest, Nottinghamshire. His character and
mode of life are well described in Scott's *Ivanhoe*. Wordsworth
aptly styles him "the English ballad-singer's joy." Upwards of forty
ballads make up the Robin Hood cycle, eight of them of the finest
quality of ballad poetry. In the *Polyolbion* of Drayton occurs this
interesting reference to Robin Hood:

> In this our spacious Isle, I think there is not one
> But he of Robin Hood hath heard, and Little John;
> And to the end of time the tales shall ne'er be done
> Of Scarlock, George a Green, and Mudge, the miller's son,
> Of Tuck, the merry friar, which many a sermon made
> In praise of Robin Hood, his outlaws, and their trade.

108–109. carelessly: free from care.

109. the golden world. Of this fabled golden age, — an ancient
and very general tradition wherein the state of man in Paradise
appears to have been shadowed, — some notion is given in Gonzalo's
commonwealth, *The Tempest*, II, i.

CHARLES. Marry, do I, sir; and I came to acquaint you with a matter. I am given, sir, secretly to understand that your younger brother, Orlando, hath a disposition to come in disguis'd against me to try a fall. To-morrow, sir, I wrestle for my credit; and he that escapes me without some broken limb shall acquit him well. Your brother is but young and tender; and, for your love, I would be loth to foil him, as I must, for my own honour, if he come in: therefore, out of my love to you, I came hither to acquaint you withal; that either you might stay him from his intendment, or brook such disgrace well as he shall run into, in that it is a thing of his own search, and altogether against my will.

OLIVER. Charles, I thank thee for thy love to me, which thou shalt find I will most kindly requite. I had myself notice of my brother's purpose herein, and have by underhand means labour'd to dissuade him from it; but he is resolute. I 'll tell thee, Charles, it is the stubbornest young fellow of France; full of ambition, an envious emulator of every man's good parts, a secret and villainous contriver against me his natural brother: therefore use thy discretion; I had as lief thou didst break his neck as his finger. And thou wert best look to 't; for if thou dost him any slight disgrace, or if he do not mightily grace himself on thee, he will practise against thee by poison, entrap thee by some treacherous device, and never leave thee till he hath ta'en thy life by some indirect means or other; for, I assure thee,

116. shall acquit him: must acquit himself. 'Shall' here retains the notion of compulsion. See Abbott, § 315.

120. withal: with it. See Abbott, § 196.

125–126. underhand: indirect, secret.

133. grace himself on thee: get himself honor or reputation at your expense. Cf. V, ii, 54; *Henry V*, III, vi, 71.

and almost with tears I speak it, there is not one so young and so villainous this day living. I speak but brotherly of him; but, should I anatomize him to thee as he is, I must blush and weep, and thou must look pale and wonder.   140

CHARLES. I am heartily glad I came hither to you. If he come to-morrow, I 'll give him his payment: if ever he go alone again, I 'll never wrestle for prize more: and so, God keep your worship!   144

OLIVER. Farewell, good Charles. [*Exit* CHARLES] — Now will I stir this gamester: I hope I shall see an end of him; for my soul, yet I know not why, hates nothing more than he. Yet he 's gentle; never school'd, and yet learn'd; full of noble device; of all sorts enchantingly belov'd; and indeed so much in the heart of the world, and especially of my own people, who best know him, that I am altogether mispris'd. But it shall not be so long; this wrestler shall clear all: nothing remains but that I kindle the boy thither; which now I 'll go about.   [*Exit*]

---

139. **anatomize** F8F4 | anathomize F1F2.   145. OLIVER | omitted in F1.

139. **anatomize.** As the word is here used, it means 'unfold,' 'explain,' or 'expose a thing thoroughly.' The word 'anatomy' was often so used. Burton's *Anatomy of Melancholy* is a capital instance in point.

142. **payment:** punishment. Still used colloquially in this sense.

146. **gamester.** Not necessarily a gambler, but a sporting character, or one sowing his wild oats. Here the word undoubtedly connotes the idea of Orlando's desire to enter the wrestling match.

148–149. "In a copy of the Fourth Folio which formerly belonged to Steevens, he has marked these lines as descriptive of Shakespeare himself." — Clar. — **gentle:** well-born. — **of noble device:** of worthy plans. For the various meanings of 'device,' see Century.

152. **mispris'd:** underestimated. So in ii, 162. Cf. 'misprision,' in *Sonnets*, LXXXVII, 11: "So thy great gift, upon misprision growing."

153. **kindle:** incite. Cf. *Macbeth*, I, iii, 121.

SCENE II. *Lawn before the* DUKE'S *palace*

Enter ROSALIND *and* CELIA

CELIA. I pray thee, Rosalind, sweet my coz, be merry.

ROSALIND. Dear Celia, I show more mirth than I am mistress of; and would you yet I were merrier? Unless you could teach me to forget a banish'd father, you must not learn me how to remember any extraordinary pleasure.   5

CELIA. Herein I see thou lov'st me not with the full weight that I love thee. If my uncle, thy banish'd father, had banish'd thy uncle, the Duke my father, so thou hadst been still with me, I could have taught my love to take thy father for mine: so wouldst thou, if the truth of thy love to me were so righteously temper'd as mine is to thee.   11

ROSALIND. Well, I will forget the condition of my estate, to rejoice in yours.   13

CELIA. You know my father hath no child but I, nor none is like to have: and, truly, when he dies, thou shalt be his heir; for what he hath taken away from thy father perforce, I will render thee again in affection; by mine honour, I will; and when I break that oath, let me turn monster: therefore, my sweet Rose, my dear Rose, be merry.

SCENE II | Scene IV Pope.　　　　　3. yet I were Rowe | yet were Ff.
CELIA | Cellia F1.　　　　　　　　5. any F1 | my F3F4.

1. **sweet my coz**: my sweet cousin. See Abbott, § 13.

5. **learn**: teach. This usage, still prevalent in Scotland and in New England, was common in Elizabethan and in Middle English, e.g. in the Miles Coverdale version of the *Psalms*, preserved with few changes in the Book of Common Prayer. Cf. Tennyson's "learn'd me Magic" in *Merlin and the Gleam*.

14. **but I.** See Abbott, § 209. — **14–15. nor none.** See Abbott, § 406.

ROSALIND. From henceforth I will, coz, and devise sports. Let me see; what think you of falling in love? 21

CELIA. Marry, I prithee, do, to make sport withal: but love no man in good earnest; nor no further in sport neither than with safety of a pure blush thou mayst in honour come off again. 25

ROSALIND. What shall be our sport, then?

CELIA. Let us sit and mock the good housewife Fortune from her wheel, that her gifts may henceforth be bestow'd equally. 29

ROSALIND. I would we could do so; for her benefits are mightily misplac'd; and the bountiful blind woman doth most mistake in her gifts to women. 32

CELIA. 'T is true; for those that she makes fair she scarce makes honest; and those that she makes honest, she makes very ill-favouredly. 35

ROSALIND. Nay, now thou goest from Fortune's office to Nature's: Fortune reigns in gifts of the world, not in the lineaments of Nature. 38

Enter TOUCHSTONE

CELIA. No? when Nature hath made a fair creature, may she not by Fortune fall into the fire? Though Nature hath

39. *Enter* TOUCHSTONE | Enter Clowne Ff.   39. **No**? Hanmer | No! Theobald | No; Ff.

27. Drive the good dame Fortune from her wheel with gibes and flouts. Cf. *Antony and Cleopatra*, IV, xv, 44; *Henry V*, III, vi, 35.
34. **honest**: virtuous. So in III, iii, 26, and elsewhere.
35. In previous editions of Hudson's Shakespeare, Rowe's emendation, 'ill-favoured,' was adopted; but the adverb expressing state or condition has here, as often in Shakespeare, the force of an adjective. In IV, iii, 86, 'favour' refers to personal appearance.

given us wit to flout at Fortune, hath not Fortune sent in
this fool to cut off the argument?   42

ROSALIND. Indeed, there is Fortune too hard for Nature, when Fortune makes Nature's natural the cutter-off
of Nature's wit.   45

CELIA. Peradventure this is not Fortune's work neither,
but Nature's; who perceiveth our natural wits too dull to
reason of such goddesses, hath sent this natural for our
whetstone; for always the dulness of the fool is the whetstone of the wits. — How now, wit! whither wander you?

TOUCHSTONE. Mistress, you must come away to your father.

CELIA. Were you made the messenger?   52

TOUCHSTONE. No, by mine honour; but I was bid to
come for you.

ROSALIND. Where learn'd you that oath, fool?   55

TOUCHSTONE. Of a certain knight that swore by his
honour they were good pancakes, and swore by his honour
the mustard was naught: now I'll stand to it, the pancakes
were naught, and the mustard was good; and yet was not
the knight forsworn.   60

CELIA. How prove you that, in the great heap of your
knowledge?

ROSALIND. Ay, marry, now unmuzzle your wisdom.

43. there is Fortune F1F2 | For-
tune is there F3F4.
47. perceiveth F1 | perceiving F2
F3F4.

48. hath sent Ff | and hath sent
Malone Camb.
50. whither F2 | whether F1.
63. your F1 | you F2.

48. Four times Shakespeare uses 'natural' in the sense of 'idiot':
The Tempest, III, ii, 37; *Romeo and Juliet*, II, iv, 96, and in the two
passages in this scene. The word is still used in the same way in Scotland. Cf. the Elizabethan use of the noun 'innocent.' The application of 'fool' to the professional clown gave rise to many quibbles.

TOUCHSTONE. Stand you both forth now : stroke your
chins, and swear by your beards that I am a knave.   65

CELIA. By our beards, if we had them, thou art.

TOUCHSTONE. By my knavery, if I had it, then I were ;
but, if you swear by that that is not, you are not forsworn :
no more was this knight, swearing by his honour, for he
never had any ; or if he had, he had sworn it away before
ever he saw those pancakes or that mustard.   71

CELIA. Prithee, who is 't that thou mean'st ?

TOUCHSTONE. One that old Frederick, your father, loves.

CELIA. My father's love is enough to honour him enough :
speak no more of him ; you 'll be whipp'd for taxation one
of these days.   76

TOUCHSTONE. The more pity, that fools may not speak
wisely what wise men do foolishly.

---

74. CELIA Theobald | Rosa-   honour him : enough ! Hanmer.
lind Ff.   78. wise men F₃F₄ | wisemen
74. honour him enough Ff | F₁F₂.

73. old. This, like ' Mistress ' in l. 51, is merely a term of familiar-
ity, such as jesters were privileged to use to all sorts of people.

74. The Folios give this speech to Rosalind, but as it was Celia's
father whose name was Frederick (V, iv, 148), Theobald conjectured
that the speech should be given to her, unless ' Frederick ' be changed
to another name. Capell proposed the substitution of ' Ferdinand.'

75. taxation : censure, satire. Cf. ' tax,' II, vii, 71 ; ' taxing,' II,
vii, 86. ' To tax,' from Lat. *taxare* (*tangere*) through Old Fr. *taxer*,
passes naturally from the meaning ' to assess ' or ' to task,' to that
of ' to take to task,' ' to censure,' ' to satirize.' ' Task ' is etymologically the same word. It was the custom to whip professional
jesters when they used their tongues too freely.

78. wise men. " There can be no doubt that the words ' wise men,'
here printed as two in obedience to modern usage, were frequently
in Shakespeare's time written and pronounced as one word, with the
accent on the first syllable, as ' madman ' is still." — Camb.

CELIA. By my troth, thou sayest true; for since the
little wit that fools have was silenc'd, the little foolery that
wise men have makes a great show. Here comes Monsieur
Le Beau.   82

ROSALIND. With his mouth full of news.

CELIA. Which he will put on us, as pigeons feed their
young.

ROSALIND. Then shall we be news-cramm'd.   86

CELIA. All the better; we shall be the more marketable. —

Enter LE BEAU

Bon jour, Monsieur Le Beau: what's the news?

LE BEAU. Fair princess, you have lost much good sport.

CELIA. Sport! of what colour?   90

LE BEAU. What colour, madam! how shall I answer you?

ROSALIND. As wit and fortune will.

TOUCHSTONE. Or as the Destinies decrees.

CELIA. Well said: that was laid on with a trowel.

82. Le Beau Steevens | the Beu
F1 | Le Beu F2F3F4. — F1 has here
'Enter Le Beau.'
83. Scene V Pope.

88. Bon | Boon Ff. — what's the
F1 | what the F2 | what F3F4.
89. Two lines in F1.

80. Fleay suggests that this may have reference to the burning of
satirical books by public authority, June 1, 1599.

90. Celia glances, apparently, at Le Beau's affected or dandified
pronunciation of 'sport,' he having got it nearer to 'spot' than to
'sport.' But 'colour' may mean 'kind,' as in III, ii, 385. Cf. *King
Lear*, II, ii, 145: "a fellow of the self-same colour."

93. **Destinies decrees.** Pope's emendation was 'decree,' adopted
in previous editions of Hudson's Shakespeare. For grammatical construction, see Abbott, § 333. The Destinies shape the speech of
those who have not sense enough to shape it for themselves.

94. **laid on with a trowel.** 'To lay on with a trowel' is a proverbial phrase, meaning to do anything lavishly or without delicacy.

TOUCHSTONE. Nay, if I keep not my rank, —   95
ROSALIND. Thou losest thy old smell.

LE BEAU. You amaze me, ladies : I would have told you
of good wrestling, which you have lost the sight of.

ROSALIND. Yet tell us the manner of the wrestling.   99

LE BEAU. I will tell you the beginning; and, if it please
your ladyships, you may see the end ; for the best is yet to
do ; and here, where you are, they are coming to perform it.

CELIA. Well, — the beginning, that is dead and buried.

LE BEAU. There comes an old man and his three sons, —

CELIA. I could match this beginning with an old tale.

LE BEAU. Three proper young men, of excellent growth
and presence.   107

ROSALIND. With bills on their necks, ' Be it known unto
all men by these presents.'   109

LE BEAU. The eldest of the three wrestled with Charles,
the Duke's wrestler ; which Charles in a moment threw
him, and broke three of his ribs, that there is little hope of
life in him : so he serv'd the second, and so the third.
Yonder they lie ; the poor old man, their father, making

96. losest F4 | loosest F1F2F3.

106. **proper**: comely. So in sixteenth century literature very often.
108. **With bills on their necks.** In previous editions of Hudson's
Shakespeare these words were given to Le Beau. This was Farmer's
emendation, and it has been defended as giving additional point and
piquancy to the pun on ' bills,' and balancing more evenly the quibble
on ' presence ' and ' presents.' ' Bills ' were instruments or weapons
used by watchmen and foresters. Watchmen were said to carry
their bills or halberds on their necks, not on their shoulders. For
example, in Lodge's *Rosalynde*, Rosader is described as " pacing . . .
with his forest-bill on his neck." The usual preamble of legal 'bills,'
or public notices, is " Be it known unto all men by these presents,"
a translation of *Noverint universi per praesentes*.

such pitiful dole over them, that all the beholders take his
part with weeping.   116

ROSALIND. Alas !

TOUCHSTONE. But what is the sport, monsieur, that the
ladies have lost?

LE BEAU. Why, this that I speak of.   120

TOUCHSTONE. Thus men may grow wiser every day : it
is the first time that ever I heard breaking of ribs was
sport for ladies.

CELIA. Or I, I promise thee.   124

ROSALIND. But is there any else longs to see this broken
music in his sides? is there yet another dotes upon rib-
breaking? — Shall we see this wrestling, cousin?   127

LE BEAU. You must, if you stay here ; for here is the place
appointed for the wrestling, and they are ready to perform it.

CELIA. Yonder, sure, they are coming : let us now stay
and see it.   131

---

125. see Ff | set Theobald | feel Dyce.   129. for the F1 | for F2F3F4.

125. see. "'See' is the colloquial term for perception or experi-
ment."— Johnson. — 125-126. broken music. Chappell, in his *Popular
Music of the Olden Time*, says this phrase means "what we now term
a string band." His later explanation, given to Dr. W. A. Wright, is :
"Some instruments, such as viols, violins, flutes, etc., were formerly
made in sets of four, which when played together formed a 'consort.'
If one or more of the instruments of one set were substituted for the
corresponding ones of another set, the result was no longer a 'consort,' but 'broken music.'" The expression occurs in *Henry V*, V,
ii, 263 : "Come, your answer in broken music ; for thy voice is music
and thy English broken." And Bacon, *Essays*, XXXVII, *Of Masques
and Triumphs :* "I understand it, that the Song be in Quire, placed
aloft, and accompanied with some broken Musicke." The implied
comparison of 'broken ribs' to 'broken music' appears to be but a
whimsical fancy, with no link of connection but a verbal one suggested by 'broken.'

Flourish.   Enter DUKE FREDERICK, Lords, ORLANDO,
CHARLES, *and* Attendants

DUKE FREDERICK. Come on : since the youth will not
be entreated, his own peril on his forwardness.

ROSALIND. Is yonder the man?

LE BEAU. Even he, madam.   135

CELIA. Alas, he is too young ! yet he looks successfully.

DUKE FREDERICK. How now, daughter, and cousin ! are
you crept hither to see the wrestling?

ROSALIND. Ay, my liege, so please you give us leave. 139

DUKE FREDERICK. You will take little delight in it, I
can tell you, there is such odds in the man. In pity of the
challenger's youth, I would fain dissuade him, but he will
not be entreated. Speak to him, ladies; see if you can
move him.   144

CELIA. Call him hither, good Monsieur Le Beau.

DUKE FREDERICK. Do so : I 'll not be by.

---

132. Scene VI Pope.   141. man Ff | men Hanmer.

133. **be entreated** : yield to entreaty, be persuaded.

136. **looks successfully**: has the appearance of one likely to suc-
ceed. Here, as in l. 35, the adverb expressing state or condition has
the force of an adjective. Cf. *The Tempest*, III, i, 32.

137. **cousin.** This word was used indifferently of nephews, nieces,
and grandchildren, as well as for what we mean by the term. Shakespeare is full of instances in point. Rosalind is niece to Frederick.

141. Hanmer substituted 'men' for the Folio reading 'man.' But
there is no necessity for such a change, as 'odds' in Elizabethan
literature often means 'superiority.' Cf. *Love's Labour 's Lost*, I, ii,
183: ". . . too much odds for a Spaniard's rapier." So in Sylvester's
translation of Du Bartas :

> No (silly lad), no, wert thou of the Gods,
> I would not fight at so unknightly odds.

LE BEAU. Monsieur the challenger, the princess calls for you.

ORLANDO. I attend them with all respect and duty.   149

ROSALIND. Young man, have you challeng'd Charles the wrestler?

ORLANDO. No, fair princess ; he is the general challenger : I come but in, as others do, to try with him the strength of my youth.   154

CELIA. Young gentleman, your spirits are too bold for your years. You have seen cruel proof of this man's strength : if you saw yourself with your eyes, or knew yourself with your judgment, the fear of your adventure would counsel you to a more equal enterprise. We pray you, for your own sake, to embrace your own safety, and give over this attempt. 160

ROSALIND. Do, young sir ; your reputation shall not therefore be mispris'd : we will make it our suit to the Duke that the wrestling might not go forward.   163

147. **princess calls** F4 | Princesse cals F1 | Princesse calls F2F3 | princesses call Theobald | princess' call Dyce.

149. **them** Ff | her Rowe.
157-158. **your eyes . . . your judgment** Ff | our eyes . . . our judgment Hanmer.

147. Most of the textual variations arise from Orlando's answer, "I attend them. . . ." But while Celia alone has expressly called for him, she is clearly speaking both for Rosalind and for herself.

157-158. In previous editions of Hudson's Shakespeare, Hanmer's emendation, "our eyes . . . our judgment," was adopted as one of many instances of words repeated by mistake from contextual nearness. The best defense of the Folio reading is Heath's paraphrase of the line: "If you would give credit to the faithful report of your own eyes, and to the cool dictates of your judgment, rather than suffer yourself to be seduced by the bold spirits of your youth."

162. So, in the first scene, Oliver, muttering to himself of his brother's popularity, shows his envy by saying, "I am altogether mispris'd."

ORLANDO. I beseech you, punish me not with your hard thoughts; wherein I confess me much guilty, to deny so fair and excellent ladies any thing: but let your fair eyes and gentle wishes go with me to my trial; wherein if I be foil'd, there is but one sham'd that was never gracious; if kill'd, but one dead that is willing to be so. I shall do my friends no wrong, for I have none to lament me; the world no injury, for in it I have nothing; only in the world I fill up a place, which may be better supplied when I have made it empty.   173

ROSALIND. The little strength that I have, I would it were with you.

CELIA. And mine, to eke out hers.

ROSALIND. Fare you well: pray heaven I be deceiv'd in you!   178

CELIA. Your heart's desires be with you!

CHARLES. Come, where is this young gallant that is so desirous to lie with his mother earth?

ORLANDO. Ready, sir; but his will hath in it a more modest working.   183

DUKE FREDERICK. You shall try but one fall.

CHARLES. No, I warrant your Grace, you shall not entreat him to a second, that have so mightily persuaded him from a first.   187

165. thoughts; wherein I F1 | thoughts. Herein I Dyce | thoughts. thoughts. Therein I Johnson | I Spedding.

165. In previous editions of Hudson's Shakespeare, 'wherein' was omitted as having no coherence with the context. In the present edition the Folio text is restored. Grammatically, 'wherein' is a *crux*, but the meaning is obvious enough. — to deny: in denying.

168. gracious: favored. The word means 'attractive' and so passes naturally into the sense of 'acceptable.' Cf. *3 Henry VI*, III, iii, 117.

ORLANDO. You mean to mock me after; you should not
have mock'd me before : but come your ways.

ROSALIND. Now Hercules be thy speed, young man ! 190

CELIA. I would I were invisible, to catch the strong fellow
by the leg.   [CHARLES *and* ORLANDO *wrestle*]

ROSALIND. O excellent young man !

CELIA. If I had a thunderbolt in mine eye, I can tell who
should down.   [CHARLES *is thrown. Shout*]

DUKE FREDERICK. No more, no more.   196

ORLANDO. Yes, I beseech your Grace : I am not yet well
breath'd.

DUKE FREDERICK. How dost thou, Charles?

LE BEAU. He cannot speak, my lord.   200

DUKE FREDERICK. Bear him away. —

                          What is thy name, young man?

ORLANDO. Orlando, my liege ; the youngest son of Sir
Rowland de Boys.

DUKE FREDERICK. I would thou hadst been son to some
            man else.

The world esteem'd thy father honourable,   205
But I did find him still mine enemy :
Thou shouldst have better pleas'd me with this deed,

188. Theobald's suggestion that this line should read, "An you
mean . . ." was adopted in previous editions of Hudson's Shakespeare. Mason proposed, "If you mean. . . ." The editors of the
Cambridge Shakespeare say : " Before we were aware of Mason's
conjecture, it occurred to us that the sentence would run better
thus : 'An you mean. . . .' 'And' for 'an' is a more probable reading
than 'if,' as it may have been omitted by the printer, who mistook
it for part of the stage direction — 'Orl. and' for 'Orland.'"

198. **breath'd** : exercised. Cf. *The Taming of the Shrew*, Ind., ii, 50.

206. **still** : always. So in III, ii, 50, and elsewhere in Shakespeare.

207. **shouldst** : wouldst. See Abbott, § 322.

Hadst thou descended from another house.
But fare thee well; thou art a gallant youth:
I would thou hadst told me of another father.   210

        [*Exeunt* DUKE FREDERICK, *train, and* LE BEAU]

CELIA. Were I my father, coz, would I do this?

ORLANDO. I am more proud to be Sir Rowland's son,
His youngest son; and would not change that calling,
To be adopted heir to Frederick.

ROSALIND. My father lov'd Sir Rowland as his soul,   215
And all the world was of my father's mind:
Had I before known this young man his son,
I should have given him tears unto entreaties,
Ere he should thus have ventur'd.

CELIA.   Gentle cousin,
Let us go thank him and encourage him: 220
My father's rough and envious disposition
Sticks me at heart. — Sir, you have well deserv'd:
If you do keep your promises in love
But justly, as you have exceeded all promise,
Your mistress shall be happy.

ROSALIND.   Gentleman,   225
        [*Giving him a chain from her neck*]

211. Scene VII Pope.
224. **as you have exceeded all
promise** Ff | as you have exceeded
promise Capell | as you've here
exceeded promise Hanmer.
225. [*Giving him* . . .] Theobald.

213. **calling**: name. A very unusual use of the word.
218. **unto**: in addition to. Cf. *Richard II*, V, iii, 97.
221. **envious**: malicious. Cf. *Love's Labour's Lost*, I, i, 100.
222. **Sticks me at heart**: stabs me to the heart.
224. In previous editions of Hudson's Shakespeare the Capell
reading was adopted, as the 'all' of the Folios seemed to upset the
metre. But the line as it stands in the text presents no greater difficulties prosodically than **many** blank verse **lines** in Shakespeare.

Wear this for me, one out of suits with fortune,
That could give more, but that her hand lacks means. —
Shall we go, coz?

    CELIA.   Ay. — Fare you well, fair gentleman.

    ORLANDO. Can I not say, I thank you? My better parts
Are all thrown down; and that which here stands up   230
Is but a quintain, a mere lifeless block.

    ROSALIND. He calls us back: my pride fell with my
           fortunes;
I 'll ask him what he would. — Did you call, sir? —
Sir, you have wrestled well, and overthrown
More than your enemies.

    CELIA.   Will you go, coz?   235

    ROSALIND. Have with you. — Fare you well.

                               [Exeunt ROSALIND *and* CELIA]

    226. one out of suits: one thrown off or discarded by fortune.
There is an obvious play here upon the word 'suit' as meaning both
'favor sued for' and 'livery.' See 'suit' and 'suite' in Century.

    231. quintain. This was a figure set up for tilters to run at in a
mock tournament. The usual form was a post with a crossbar fixed
to the top, turning on a pivot, having a broad board at one end and a
bag full of sand at the other. Sometimes the figure was the, likeness
of a Saracen, or a Turk, with a sword in the right hand and a shield
on the left arm. The skill consisted in striking the quintain dexter-
ously on the broad board, or target, and then dodging the blow of
the sand bag, or sword, as it whirled round. There are the remains of
an old quintain near Maidstone in Kent; and at the May games held
at St. Mary Cray (Kentshire) in 1891 the quintain was revived. Orlando
is talking to himself in this speech, the ladies having withdrawn.

    234-235. Tennyson regarded these two lines as "one of the most
exquisite things for simplicity and eloquence in Shakespeare." —
Memoir, by Hallam Lord Tennyson, II, 153.

    236. Have with you: I will go along with you. An expression in
colloquial use in England as late as the close of the eighteenth century.

ORLANDO. What passion hangs these weights upon my
      tongue?
I cannot speak to her, yet she urg'd conference.
O poor Orlando, thou art overthrown!
Or Charles or something weaker masters thee.   240

Re-enter LE BEAU   *Monday*

LE BEAU. Good sir, I do in friendship counsel you
To leave this place. Albeit you have deserv'd
High commendation, true applause, and love,
Yet such is now the Duke's condition,
That he misconstrues all that you have done.   245
The Duke is humorous: what he is, indeed,
More suits you to conceive than I to speak of.
    ORLANDO. I thank you, sir: and, pray you, tell me this;
Which of the two was daughter of the Duke,
That here was at the wrestling?   250

---

240. Ff have *Enter* . . . after l. 238.   245. misconstrues | misconsters Ff.

244. condition: disposition. Shakespeare often uses this word in
the sense of 'disposition,' or 'temper.' So in *The Merchant of Venice*,
I, ii, 143, Portia says of the Moorish prince who comes to woo her,
"If he have the condition of a saint, and the complexion of a devil,
I had rather he should shrive me than wive me." Cf. *Richard III*,
IV, iv, 157, "Madam, I have a touch of your condition."

246. humorous: crotchety, capricious, moody, subject to fits and
starts. The word comes to have this meaning from the theory of
the old physiologists that four cardinal humors — blood, choler or
yellow bile, phlegm, and melancholy or black bile — determine, by
their conditions and proportions, a person's physical and mental
qualities. The influence of this theory survives in the application of
the terms 'sanguine,' 'choleric,' 'phlegmatic,' and 'melancholy' to
disposition and temperament. See Furness for a suggestive note.

LE BEAU. Neither his daughter, if we judge by manners,
But yet, indeed, the taller is his daughter:
The other is daughter to the banish'd Duke,
And here detain'd by her usurping uncle,
To keep his daughter company; whose loves   255
Are dearer than the natural bond of sisters.
But I can tell you, that of late this Duke
Hath ta'en displeasure 'gainst his gentle niece,
Grounded upon no other argument
But that the people praise her for her virtues,   260
And pity her for her good father's sake;
And, on my life, his malice 'gainst the lady
Will suddenly break forth. Sir, fare you well:
Hereafter, in a better world than this,
I shall desire more love and knowledge of you.   265

ORLANDO. I rest much bounden to you: fare you well.

[*Exit* LE BEAU]

Thus must I from the smoke into the smother;
From tyrant Duke unto a tyrant brother:—
But heavenly Rosalind!   [*Exit*]

252. taller. In the light of I, iii, 111, and IV, iii, 87, this description of Celia is obviously a mistake. In Shakespeare there are many
surface inconsistencies of this kind. Malone substituted 'smaller';
Rowe, 'shorter,'—the reading adopted in previous editions of Hudson's Shakespeare. Spedding suggested 'lesser,' and this was followed in the Globe edition. Walker suspected 'taller' to be "a
slip of Shakespeare's pen," and adds, "the word he had in his
thoughts was probably 'shorter,' not 'smaller,' which in this sense
belongs to later English."

264. in a better world than this: in a better state of things than
the present. No allusion to the world beyond the grave.

267. from the smoke into the smother: from bad to worse. Evidently a proverb and, like many popular saws, alliterative.

SCENE III. *A room in the palace*

Enter CELIA *and* ROSALIND

CELIA. Why, cousin! why, Rosalind! Cupid have mercy!
— not a word?

ROSALIND. Not one to throw at a dog.

CELIA. No, thy words are too precious to be cast away
upon curs; throw some of them at me; come, lame me
with reasons.   6

ROSALIND. Then there were two cousins laid up; when
the one should be lam'd with reasons, and the other mad
without any.

CELIA. But is all this for your father?   10

ROSALIND. No, some of it is for my child's father. O,
how full of briers is this working-day world!

CELIA. They are but burs, cousin, thrown upon thee in
holiday foolery: if we walk not in the trodden paths, our
very petticoats will catch them.   15

ROSALIND. I could shake them off my coat: these burs
are in my heart.

CELIA. Hem them away.

ROSALIND. I would try, if I could cry hem, and have him.

CELIA. Come, come, wrestle with thy affections.   20

ROSALIND. O, they take the part of a better wrestler than
myself!

CELIA. O, a good wish upon you! you will try in time,
in despite of a fall. But, turning these jests out of service,

SCENE III | Scene VIII Pope.   11. **child's father** Ff | father's
4. **thy** F_1F_2 | my F_3F_4.   child Rowe Pope Johnson Dyce.

24. A quibble is probably intended between falling in love and
falling by a wrestler's hand.

let us talk in good earnest. Is it possible, on such a sudden, you should fall into so strong a liking with old Sir Rowland's youngest son?   27

ROSALIND. The Duke my father lov'd his father dearly.

CELIA. Doth it therefore ensue that you should love his son dearly? By this kind of chase, I should hate him, for my father hated his father dearly; yet I hate not Orlando.

ROSALIND. No, faith, hate him not, for my sake.   32

CELIA. Why should I not? doth he not deserve well?

ROSALIND. Let me love him for that; and do you love him because I do. Look, here comes the Duke.

CELIA. With his eyes full of anger.   36

Enter DUKE FREDERICK, *with* Lords

DUKE FREDERICK. Mistress, dispatch you with your safest haste,
And get you from our court.

ROSALIND.   Me, uncle?

DUKE FREDERICK.   You, cousin;
Within these ten days if that thou be'st found
So near our public court as twenty miles,   40
Thou diest for it.

26. strong F₁F₂ | strange F₃F₄.   37. *Enter . . .* | Enter Duke with
33. Scene IX Pope.   Lords Ff (after l. 33).

31. In Shakespeare's time it was just as correct to speak of hating dearly as of loving dearly; to speak of a dear foe as well of a dear friend. So in *Hamlet*, I, ii, 182:

> Would I had met my dearest foe in heaven,
> Or ever I had seen that day.

33. Celia here speaks ironically, her meaning apparently being: It was because your father deserved well that my father hated him; and ought I not, by your reasoning, to hate Orlando for the same cause?

ROSALIND.   I do beseech your Grace,
Let me the knowledge of my fault bear with me :
If with myself I hold intelligence,
Or have acquaintance with mine own desires ;
If that I do not dream, or be not frantic, —   45
As I do trust I am not, — then, dear uncle,
Never so much as in a thought unborn
Did I offend your Highness.

DUKE FREDERICK.   Thus do all traitors :
If their purgation did consist in words,
They are as innocent as grace itself :   50
Let it suffice thee, that I trust thee not.

ROSALIND. Yet your mistrust cannot make me a traitor :
Tell me whereon the likelihood depends.

DUKE FREDERICK. Thou art thy father's daughter ; there 's
        enough.

ROSALIND. So was I when your Highness took his duke-
        dom ;   55
So was I when your Highness banish'd him :
Treason is not inherited, my lord ;
Or, if we did derive it from our friends,
What 's that to me ? my father was no traitor :
Then, good my liege, mistake me not so much   60
To think my poverty is treacherous.

CELIA. Dear sovereign, hear me speak.

DUKE FREDERICK. Ay, Celia ; we stay'd her for your sake,
Else had she with her father rang'd along.

53. likelihood F₂F₃F₄ | likelihoods F₁.   59. me ? Theobald | me, Ff.

49. purgation : proof of innocence. Dr. Furness points out that this
is a technical use of a legal term, vulgar purgation, as distinguished
from canonical, demanding ordeals by fire, water, or combat.

CELIA. I did not then entreat to have her stay;   65
It was your pleasure and your own remorse:
I was too young that time to value her;
But now I know her: if she be a traitor,
Why, so am I; we still have slept together,
Rose at an instant, learn'd, play'd, eat together;   70
And wheresoe'er we went, like Juno's swans,
Still we went coupled and inseparable.

DUKE FREDERICK. She is too subtle for thee; and her
            smoothness,
Her very silence, and her patience,
Speak to the people, and they pity her.   75
Thou art a fool: she robs thee of thy name;
And thou wilt show more bright and seem more virtuous
When she is gone. Then open not thy lips:
Firm and irrevocable is my doom
Which I have pass'd upon her: she is banish'd.   80

CELIA. Pronounce that sentence, then, on me, my liege:
I cannot live out of her company.

DUKE FREDERICK. You are a fool. — You, niece, provide
            yourself:
If you outstay the time, upon mine honour,
And in the greatness of my word, you die.   85

[*Exeunt* DUKE FREDERICK *and* Lords]

CELIA. O my poor Rosalind! whither wilt thou go?
Wilt thou change fathers? I will give thee mine.
I charge thee, be not thou more griev'd than I am.

---

86. Scene X Pope.   87. fathers F_1 | father $F_2F_3F_4$.

66. **remorse**: compassion. So in *The Tempest*, V, i, 77.

71. **Juno's swans.** Commentators make clear that it was Venus and not Juno who had the "coupled swans."

ROSALIND. I have more cause.

CELIA.   Thou hast not, cousin.
Prithee, be cheerful : know'st thou not, the Duke   90
Hath banish'd me, his daughter?

ROSALIND.   That he hath not.

CELIA. No, hath not? Rosalind lacks, then, the love
Which teacheth thee that thou and I am one :
Shall we be sunder'd? shall we part, sweet girl?
No ; let my father seek another heir.   95
Therefore devise with me how we may fly,
Whither to go, and what to bear with us :
And do not seek to take your change upon you,
To bear your griefs yourself, and leave me out ;
For, by this heaven, now at our sorrows pale,   100
Say what thou canst, I 'll go along with thee.

ROSALIND. Why, whither shall we go?

CELIA. To seek my uncle in the forest of Arden.

ROSALIND. Alas, what danger will it be to us,
Maids as we are, to travel forth so far !   105
Beauty provoketh thieves sooner than gold.

CELIA. I 'll put myself in poor and mean attire,
And with a kind of umber smirch my face;

92. **No,** Ff | No? Rowe.
93. **thee** Ff | me Theobald. —
thou Ff | she Capell (conj.). — **am**
Ff | are Hanmer.

98. **your change** F1 | your charge
F2F3F4.
108. **smirch** F1 | smitch F2 | smutch
F3.

93. The Folio reading is retained, as neither the sense nor the grammar warrants alteration.   Johnson's famous defense of 'thee' is : " Where would be the absurdity of saying, You know not the law which teaches you to do right ? "   Elizabethan grammar sanctions the attraction of a verb to its nearest subject.

98. **change** : altered fortune. Dr. Furness would read 'charge.'
108. **umber** : a dusky, yellow-colored earth. From Umbria in Italy

The like do you : so shall we pass along,
And never stir assailants.

ROSALIND.   Were it not better,   110
Because that I am more than common tall,
That I did suit me all points like a man?
A gallant curtle-axe upon my thigh,
A boar-spear in my hand ; and — in my heart
Lie there what hidden woman's fear there will —   115
We 'll have a swashing and a martial outside ;
As many other mannish cowards have
That do outface it with their semblances.

CELIA. What shall I call thee when thou art a man?

ROSALIND. I 'll have no worse a name than Jove's own
            page ;   120
And therefore look you call me Ganymede.
But what will you be call'd?

CELIA. Something that hath a reference to my state ;
No longer Celia, but Aliena.

ROSALIND. But, cousin, what if we assay'd to steal   125
The clownish fool out of your father's court?
Would he not be a comfort to our travel?

113. **curtle-axe.** This form of the word (Fr. *coutelas*) is a popular
corruption of the sixteenth century 'coutelase,' a short sword. Other
forms are 'courtlas,' 'curtlass,' 'curtlaxe.' Spenser, *The Faerie
Queene*, IV, ii, 42, uses the form 'curtaxe.'

116. **swashing.** So in Fuller's *Worthies of England:* "A ruffian
is the same with a swaggerer, so called, because endeavouring to
make that side swag or weigh down, whereon he engageth. The
same also with swash-buckler, from swashing or making a noise on
bucklers." 'Swashers' occurs in *Henry V*, III, ii, 30.

118. 'It' is used here indefinitely. See Abbott, § 226.

121. "Alinda being called Aliena, and Rosalynd Ganimede, they
traveiled along the vineyardes." — Lodge's *Rosalynde*.

CELIA. He 'll go along o'er the wide world with me ;
Leave me alone to woo him. Let 's away,
And get our jewels and our wealth together ;   130
Devise the fittest time and safest way
To hide us from pursuit that will be made
After my flight. Now go in we content,
To liberty, and not to banishment.   [*Exeunt*]

129. woo Rowe | woe F1 | wooe F2.   133. in we F1 | we in F2F3.

133. If the First Folio reading be followed, 'content' is an adjective. The text of the other Folios makes 'content' a noun meaning 'contentment,' as in III, ii, 24; *Henry VIII*, II, iii, 21.

ACT II

Scene I. *The Forest of Arden*

Enter Duke Senior, Amiens, *and other* Lords, *like foresters*

Duke Senior. Now, my co-mates and brothers in exile,
Hath not old custom made this life more sweet
Than that of painted pomp? Are not these woods
More free from peril than the envious court?
Here feel we not the penalty of Adam.   5
The seasons' difference, — as the icy fang
And churlish chiding of the winter's wind,

---

5. not Ff | but Theobald.—Adam. | Adam, Ff.

6. — as the icy fang | as the Icie phange Ff.

5. Here feel we not the penalty of Adam. Theobald changed the 'not' of the Folios into 'but', and has been followed by a number of editors. This puts 'season's difference' in apposition with 'penalty of Adam.' While the change of seasons was of old thought to be a consequence of the Fall, it was never thought to be the special penalty denounced upon Adam: the penalty was, "In the sweat of thy face shalt thou eat bread." The curse was held to be laid upon Adam as head and representative of the race, and most men have ever been subject to it; yet there have always been some individual exceptions, as the Duke and his co-mates are in their exile: "they fleet the time carelessly, as they did in the golden world." The Duke then goes on, consistently, to say what they do feel.

6. In previous editions of Hudson's Shakespeare this line read, 'the seasons' difference and the icy fang,' but in the present text the reading of the Folios is restored, with a readjustment of the punctuation. — **as**: namely, to wit.

34

Which when it bites and blows upon my body,
Even till I shrink with cold, I smile, and say,
' This is no flattery,' — these are counsellors   10
That feelingly persuade me what I am.
Sweet are the uses of adversity ;
Which, like the toad, ugly and venomous,
Wears yet a precious jewel in his head :
And this our life, exempt from public haunt,   15
Finds tongues in trees, books in the running brooks,
Sermons in stones and good in every thing.

    AMIENS. I would not change it. Happy is your Grace.

   8. bites F_1F_2 | baits F_3F_4.   18. I . . . it (see note below).

   8. **Which.** While this ' which ' may be explained as equivalent to
' as to which ' (Abbott, § 272), it is more obviously an example of
anacoluthon. — bites and blows : blows bitingly. A hendiadys.

   13–14. Of the twenty-three allusions (five of them significantly
enough in *Richard III*) which Shakespeare makes to the toad, about
half refer to the venom which old belief attributed to it, the others
to its ugliness. The passage in the text is the only allusion to the
toadstone of the sixteenth century naturalists. With that passion
for real or fictitious natural history which is one of the characteristics
of euphuism, Lyly says in a passage quoted word for word by Meres
in *Wits Commonwealth*, " the foule Toade hath a faire stone in his
head," and then he moralizes thereon. King, in his *Natural History
of Gems and Decorative Stones*, shows how the old belief is undoubtedly based upon a popular etymology. Referring to the Batrachites,
or toadstone, of Pliny as having received its name because it was
like the toad or frog in color, he says : " Understanding the ancient
term as implying the natural production of the animal according to
the analogy of other similar names, as the Saurites, Echites, etc.,
doctors taught that ' the toad, ugly and venomous, wears yet a precious jewel in his head.' "

   18. **I would not change it.** In the Folios these words stand as the
beginning of the speech of Amiens. Upton gave the first words to
the Duke, and Dyce observes : " It seems strange that no one before

That can translate the stubbornness of fortune
Into so quiet and so sweet a style.   20

DUKE SENIOR. Come, shall we go and kill us venison?
And yet it irks me the poor dappled fools,
Being native burghers of this desert city,
Should in their own confines with forked heads,
Have their round haunches gor'd.

FIRST LORD.   Indeed, my lord,   25
The melancholy Jaques grieves at that;
And, in that kind, swears you do more usurp
Than doth your brother that hath banish'd you.
To-day my Lord of Amiens and myself
Did steal behind him as he lay along   30
Under an oak, whose antique root peeps out

Upton should have seen that they must belong to the Duke, and
still stranger that, after the error was once pointed out, any editor
should persist in retaining it." For a defense of the reading of the
Folios, see Furness.

23. Lodge speaks of sheep as "citizens of field." He also applies
to deer the expression "citizens of wood." Cf. *The Merchant of
Venice*, I, i, 10, and Drayton's *Polyolbion*, XVIII:

> Where, feareless of the Hunt, the Hart securely stood,
> And euery where walkt free, a Burgesse of the Wood.

24. **forked heads**. Question has been made as to what these
were. Ascham, in *Toxophilus*, appears to settle the matter. He
describes two kinds of arrow heads as follows : "The one ... hauying
two poyntes or barbes, lookyng backewarde to the stele and the
fethers, which surely we call in Englishe a brode arrowe head or a
swalowe tayle. The other ... hauing .ii. poyntes stretchyng for-
warde, and this Englysh men do call a forke-head." And again :
"Commodus the Emperoure vsed forked heades, whose facion
Herodiane doeth lyuely and naturally describe, sayinge that they
were lyke the shap of a new mone." That 'forked heads' are not
'antlers' is obvious. Stags could hardly gore their own haunches.

Upon the brook that brawls along this wood :
To the which place a poor sequester'd stag,
That from the hunter's aim had ta'en a hurt,
Did come to languish ; and, indeed, my lord,   35
The wretched animal heav'd forth such groans,
That their discharge did stretch his leathern coat
Almost to bursting, and the big round tears
Cours'd one another down his innocent nose
In piteous chase ; and thus the hairy fool,   40
Much marked of the melancholy Jaques,
Stood on th' extremest verge of the swift brook,
Augmenting it with tears.

    DUKE SENIOR.   But what said Jaques?
Did he not moralize this spectacle?

    FIRST LORD. O, yes, into a thousand similes.   45
First, for his weeping into the needless stream ;
' Poor deer,' quoth he, ' thou mak'st a testament
As worldlings do, giving thy sum of more
To that which had too much.' Then, being there alone,
Left and abandon'd of his velvet friends ;   50
' 'T is right,' quoth he ; ' thus misery doth part

---

    49. there F_1 | omitted in $F_2F_3F_4$.   50. friends Rowe | friend Ff.

    43. So Drayton, in *Polyolbion*, XIII, in a spirited description of a
deer hunt in the Warwickshire forest of Arden, has these lines :

> He who the Mourner is to his owne dying Corse
> Upon the ruthless earthe his precious teares lets fall.

Attached to this is a marginal note : "The Hart weepeth at his dying ;
his teares are held to be precious in medicine."

    46. **needless** : not needing. See Abbott, § 3.
    48-49. Cf. *3 Henry VI*, V, iv, 8 ; *A Lover's Complaint*, 38-40.
    50. **velvet friends** : sleek-coated companions.

The flux of company : ' anon, a careless herd,
Full of the pasture, jumps along by him,
And never stays to greet him : 'Ay,' quoth Jaques,
'Sweep on, you fat and greasy citizens ;   55
'T is just the fashion : wherefore do you look
Upon that poor and broken bankrupt there?'
Thus most invectively he pierceth through
The body of the country, city, court,
Yea, and of this our life ; swearing that we   60
Are mere usurpers, tyrants, and what 's worse,
To fright the animals and to kill them up,
In their assign'd and native dwelling-place.

    DUKE SENIOR. And did you leave him in this contemplation?

    SECOND LORD. We did, my lord, weeping and commenting
Upon the sobbing deer.

    DUKE SENIOR.   Show me the place :   66
I love to cope him in these sullen fits,
For then he 's full of matter.

    FIRST LORD. I 'll bring you to him straight.   [*Exeunt*]

---

    59. of the $F_2F_3F_4$ | of F_1.   60. of this F_1 | this F_3F_4.

    52. flux : current. Or 'conflux,' as in *Paradise Regained*, IV, 62.

    57. Moberly suggested that Shakespeare had his father's bankruptcy in mind when he wrote this passage.

    58. invectively : in bitter terms. A very rare use of the word.

    61. what 's. 'What' is for the indefinite 'whatever.'

    62. kill them up. 'Up' in Middle and Elizabethan English is often added to verbs intensively to show that the action is completed. Cf. Chaucer, *The Legend of Good Women*, ll. 1216–1217 :

> Thus seyn thise yonge folk, and up they kille
> These hertes wilde, and han hem at his wille.

    67. cope : encounter. This verb is now used intransitively.

Scene II. *A room in the palace*

Enter Duke Frederick, *with* Lords

Duke Frederick. Can it be possible that no man saw
    them?
It cannot be : some villains of my court
Are of consent and sufferance in this.

  First Lord. I cannot hear of any that did see her.
The ladies, her attendants of her chamber,   5
Saw her a-bed ; and, in the morning early,
They found the bed untreasur'd of their mistress.

  Second Lord. My lord, the roynish clown, at whom so oft
Your Grace was wont to laugh, is also missing.
Hisperia, the princess' gentlewoman,   10
Confesses that she secretly o'erheard
Your daughter and her cousin much commend
The parts and graces of the wrestler

A room in . . . Capell.   10. **Hisperia** Ff | Hesperia Warburton.

  3. consent and sufferance. "A quasi-legal term, applied to a landlord who takes no steps to eject a tenant whose time is expired."—Moberly.

  8. roynish. The word is here used as a general term of contempt; literally it means 'scabbed,' 'mangy.' It is from the Middle English 'roigne' or 'royne,' a word found in the description of Idleness, the 'mayden curteys,' in *The Romaunt of the Rose:*

> Her nekke was of good fasoun,
> In lengthe and gretnesse, by resoun,
> Withoute bleyne, scabbe, or royne.

It is the Old French *roingne* from the Latin *robigo.* Chaucer uses the forms 'roinous,' 'roynous,' in the sense of 'rough.' From the same French and Latin sources comes 'ronyon' ('roinon,' 'runnion'), the word used by Shakespeare in *The Merry Wives of Windsor*, IV, ii, 195, and *Macbeth*, I, iii, 6.

That did but lately foil the sinewy Charles;
And she believes, wherever they are gone,   15
That youth is surely in their company.

    DUKE FREDERICK. Send to his brother; fetch that gal-
        lant hither:
If he be absent, bring his brother to me;
I 'll make him find him: do this suddenly;
And let not search and inquisition quail   20
To bring again these foolish runaways.   [*Exeunt*]

SCENE III. *Before* OLIVER'S *house*

Enter ORLANDO *and* ADAM, *meeting*

    ORLANDO. Who 's there?
    ADAM. What, my young master? O my gentle master!
O my sweet master! O you memory
Of old Sir Rowland! why, what make you here?
Why are you virtuous? why do people love you?   5
And wherefore are you gentle, strong, and valiant?
Why would you be so fond to overcome

---

    17. brother Ff | brother's Capell.   *Before* OLIVER'S *house* Capell.

    17. his brother. As 'that gallant' clearly refers to Orlando, and
as the order is to send to Oliver's house, Mason suggested the emendation, 'his brother's,' already existing in Capell's text, and this
reading was adopted in previous editions of Hudson's Shakespeare.

    20. quail: slacken. Middle English *quelen*, Anglo-Saxon *cwelan*,
'to die.'

    3. memory: memorial. In Middle and Elizabethan English the
use of abstract nouns in a concrete sense is common. So in the
Communion Service of the Episcopal Church : "A perpetual memory of that his precious death," etc.

    4. make: do. See note, p. 5, l. 26.

    7. fond: foolishly eager. For the derivation of 'fond,' see Skeat.

The bonny priser of the humorous Duke?
Your praise is come too swiftly home before you.
Know you not, master, to some kind of men   10
Their graces serve them but as enemies?
No more do yours: your virtues, gentle master,
Are sanctified and holy traitors to you.
O, what a world is this, when what is comely
Envenoms him that bears it!   15

    ORLANDO. Why, what's the matter?

    ADAM.   O unhappy youth!
Come not within these doors; within this roof
The enemy of all your graces lives:
Your brother — no, no brother; yet the son —
Yet not the son, I will not call him son   20
Of him I was about to call his father, —
Hath heard your praises; and this night he means
To burn the lodging where you use to lie,
And you within it: if he fail of that,
He will have other means to cut you off: 25

---

8. **bonny** F₂F₃F₄ | bonnie F₁ | 16. ORLANDO omitted in F₁.
boney Warburton | bony Johnson.   20. Line in parenthesis Ff.

    8. **bonny**. In previous editions of Hudson's Shakespeare, War-
burton's emendation 'boney' (or 'bony') was adopted. But 'bony'
is hardly an epithet to describe a wrestler, though 'sinewy' (II, ii,
14) may be; and to this day in the North of England and in Scotland 'bonny' is used in the sense of 'large,' 'stalwart.' — **priser**:
prize-fighter. — **humorous**: crotchety. See note, p. 25, l. 246.

    13. Shakespeare is fond of thus mixing incongruous words in
order to express certain complexities of thought. In like sort, even
so grave a writer as Richard Hooker has the expression 'heavenly
fraud' in a thoroughly good sense.

    15. **Envenoms**: poisons. Not that which makes a man venomous,
but that which acts like venom upon him.

I overheard him and his practices.
This is no place; this house is but a butchery:
Abhor it, fear it, do not enter it.

    ORLANDO. Why, whither, Adam, wouldst thou have me go?

    ADAM. No matter whither, so you come not here.   30

    ORLANDO. What, wouldst thou have me go and beg my food?
Or with a base and boisterous sword enforce
A thievish living on the common road?
This I must do, or know not what to do:
Yet this I will not do, do how I can;   35
I rather will subject me to the malice
Of a diverted blood and bloody brother.

    ADAM. But do not so. I have five hundred crowns,
The thrifty hire I sav'd under your father,
Which I did store to be my foster-nurse   40
When service should in my old limbs lie lame,
And unregarded age in corners thrown:
Take that; and He that doth the ravens feed,
Yea, providently caters for the sparrow,
Be comfort to my age! Here is the gold;   45
All this I give you. Let me be your servant:
Though I look old, yet I am strong and lusty;
For in my youth I never did apply
Hot and rebellious liquors in my blood;
Nor did not with unbashful forehead woo   50
The means of weakness and debility:
Therefore my age is as a lusty winter,

29, 30. **whither** | whether F1.   30. **so** F1 | for F2F3F4.

27. **place**: residence.—**butchery**: slaughterhouse. Cf.Fr. *boucherie.*
37. **diverted blood**: blood (i.e. affection) turned out of its natural course. Cf. 'gentle condition of blood,' I, i, 40-41.

Frosty, but kindly : let me go with you ;
I 'll do the service of a younger man
In all your business and necessities.   55
   ORLANDO. O good old man, how well in thee appears
The constant service of the antique world,
When service sweat for duty, not for meed !
Thou art not for the fashion of these times,
Where none will sweat but for promotion;   60
And, having that, do choke their service up
Even with the having; it is not so with thee.
But, poor old man, thou prun'st a rotten tree,
That cannot so much as a blossom yield
In lieu of all thy pains and husbandry.   65
But come thy ways ; we 'll go along together ;
And, ere we have thy youthful wages spent,
We 'll light upon some settled low content.
   ADAM. Master, go on, and I will follow thee,
To the last gasp, with truth and loyalty.   70
From seventeen years till now almost fourscore
Here lived I, but now live here no more.
At seventeen years many their fortunes seek ;
But at fourscore it is too late a week :
Yet fortune cannot recompense me better   75
Than to die well, and not my master's debtor.   [*Exeunt*]

58. **meed** | some copies of F1 read   71. **seventeen** Rowe | seauentie
meede, others *neede* | need F4.   F1 | seventy F2F3F4.

  53. **kindly** : natural, seasonable. Cf. ' kind,' III, ii, 95 ; IV, iii, 59.
  58. **sweat**. Past indicative. See Abbott, § 341.
  61–62. Because their promotion makes them too proud to serve.
  65. **In lieu of** : in return for. So in *The Merchant of Venice*, IV, i, 410.
  74. **a week**. Obviously a proverbial expression to signify an
indefinite period. " Equivalent to ' i' the week.' " — Clar.

SCENE IV.   *The Forest of Arden*

Enter ROSALIND *for* GANYMEDE, CELIA *for* ALIENA,
and TOUCHSTONE

ROSALIND. O Jupiter, how merry are my spirits!

TOUCHSTONE. I care not for my spirits, if my legs were
not weary.   3

ROSALIND. I could find in my heart to disgrace my
man's apparel, and to cry like a woman; but I must comfort the weaker vessel, as doublet and hose ought to show
itself courageous to petticoat: therefore, courage! good
Aliena.   8

CELIA. I pray you, bear with me; I cannot go no further.

TOUCHSTONE. For my part, I had rather bear with you
than bear you: yet I should bear no cross, if I did bear
you; for I think you have no money in your purse.   12

ROSALIND. Well, this is the forest of Arden.

---

1. **merry** Ff | weary Theobald.   9. **cannot** F₁ | can F₂F₃F₄.

1. Furness makes a brilliant defense of the Folio reading 'merry'
in Rosalind's opening speech. He says: " With all deference to my
betters, I respectfully but firmly protest against making the cart
draw the horse, and changing Rosalind's speech to suit the humor
in Touchstone's. . . . Is it not clear that Rosalind is talking for
effect? . . . Of course this merriment of hers is assumed, and that
it is assumed, and that we may know that it is assumed, she tells us,
in an aside, by confessing that in her heart she is ready to cry like
a woman."

11. In Shakespeare's time English silver coins had a cross stamped
on the reverse, and hence were called 'crosses.' This gave occasion for frequent puns. So Scott, in *Woodstock*, Chapter III:
"No devil so frightful as that which dances in the pocket where
there is no cross to keep him out." "A play upon . . . *Matthew*,
x, 38." — Clar.

TOUCHSTONE. Ay, now am I in Arden; the more fool I;
when I was at home, I was in a better place; but travellers
must be content.   16

ROSALIND. Ay, be so, good Touchstone. Look you, who
comes here; a young man and an old in solemn talk.

Enter CORIN *and* SILVIUS

CORIN. That is the way to make her scorn you still.
SILVIUS. O Corin, that thou knew'st how I do love her!
CORIN. I partly guess; for I have lov'd ere now.   21
SILVIUS. No, Corin, being old, thou canst not guess,
Though in thy youth thou wast as true a lover
As ever sigh'd upon a midnight pillow:
But if thy love were ever like to mine, —   25
As sure I think did never man love so, —
How many actions most ridiculous
Hast thou been drawn to by thy fantasy?
CORIN. Into a thousand that I have forgotten.
SILVIUS. O, thou didst then never love so heartily!   30
If thou remember'st not the slightest folly
That ever love did make thee run into,
Thou hast not lov'd:
Or if thou hast not sat as I do now,
Wearing thy hearer in thy mistress' praise,   35
Thou hast not lov'd:
Or if thou hast not broke from company

19. *Enter* . . . In Ff after l. 16.   35. Wearing F1 | Wearying F2F3F4.

18. solemn: earnest. So in *King John*, IV, ii, 90, and elsewhere.
35. Wearing: wearying. Unnecessary to adopt the Second Folio
reading.

Abruptly, as my passion now makes me,
Thou hast not lov'd.   39
O Phebe, Phebe, Phebe !   [*Exit*]

ROSALIND. Alas, poor shepherd ! searching of thy wound,
I have by hard adventure found mine own.   42

TOUCHSTONE. And I mine. I remember, when I was in
love I broke my sword upon a stone, and bid him take that
for coming a-night to Jane Smile : and I remember the
kissing of her batler and the cow's dugs that her pretty
chopt hands had milk'd : and I remember the wooing of a
peascod instead of her ; from whom I took two cods and,
giving her them again, said with weeping tears, ' Wear these
for my sake.' We that are true lovers run into strange
capers ; but as all is mortal in nature, so is all nature in
love mortal in folly.   52

ROSALIND. Thou speak'st wiser than thou art ware of.

TOUCHSTONE. Nay, I shall ne'er be ware of mine own
wit till I break my shins against it.   55

---

41. **of thy wound** Rowe | of they   45. **a-night** | a night F1 | a nights F2.
would F1 | of their wound F2F3F4.   46. **batler** F1 | batlet F2F3F4.

44. **him.** The imaginary rival for whose visits to Jane Smile the
stone was held vicariously responsible.

46. **batler** : a small bat used by washerwomen for beating clothes.
See Skeat under ' battledoor.'

47. **chopt** : chapped. So in *Julius Cæsar*, I, ii, 247; *Sonnets*,
LXII, 10.

48. **peascod** : pea pod. Pea pods were used for divination in love
affairs and for ornament. ' Whom ' may refer to Jane or to the plant.
Touchstone is humorously incoherent.

52. **mortal in folly.** Schmidt suggests the interpretation ' human
in folly,' but it is much more natural to regard ' mortal ' here as a
general intensive. This provincial use of the word is common to-day
in such phrases as ' mortal great.'

ROSALIND. Jove, Jove ! this shepherd's passion
        Is much upon my fashion.

TOUCHSTONE. And mine; but it grows something stale
    with me.

CELIA. I pray you, one of you question yond man,
If he for gold will give us any food :   60
I faint almost to death.

TOUCHSTONE.   Holla, you clown !

ROSALIND. Peace, fool : he's not thy kinsman.

CORIN.   Who calls?

TOUCHSTONE. Your betters, sir.

CORIN.   Else are they very wretched.

ROSALIND. Peace, I say. — Good even to you, friend.

CORIN. And to you, gentle sir, and to you all.   65

ROSALIND. I prithee, shepherd, if that love or gold
Can in this desert place buy entertainment,
Bring us where we may rest ourselves and feed :
Here's a young maid with travel much oppress'd
And faints for succour.

CORIN.   Fair sir, I pity her,   70
And wish, for her sake more than for mine own,
My fortunes were more able to relieve her ;
But I am shepherd to another man
And do not shear the fleeces that I graze :
My master is of churlish disposition,   75

59. **yond** Rowe | yon'd Ff.   64. **you, friend** F2F3F4 | your friend F1.

64. "One of the many instances where, in the Folio, 'you' and 'your' are confounded." — Furness.

67. **desert**: uninhabited. Often so in modern English poetry.

70. **faints for succour**: faints for want of succor. See note, p. 67, l. 28. For ellipsis of nominative, see Abbott, §§ 399–402.

And little recks to find the way to heaven·
By doing deeds of hospitality :
Besides, his cote, his flocks, and bounds of feed,
Are now on sale ; and at our sheepcote now,
By reason of his absence, there is nothing   80
That you will feed on ; but what is, come see,
And in my voice most welcome shall you be.

    ROSALIND.   What is he that shall buy his flock and pasture ?

    CORIN.   That young swain that you saw here but erewhile,
That little cares for buying any thing.   85

    ROSALIND.   I pray thee, if it stand with honesty,
Buy thou the cottage, pasture, and the flock,
And thou shalt have to pay for it of us.

    CELIA.   And we will mend thy wages.   I like this place,
And willingly could waste my time in it.   90

    CORIN.   Assuredly the thing is to be sold :
Go with me : if you like upon report
The soil, the profit, and this kind of life,
I will your very faithful feeder be,   94
And buy it with your gold right suddenly.   [*Exeunt*]

---

  76. recks Hanmer | wreakes F1
F2 | wreaks F3F4.
  78. cote Hanmer | Coate F1F2.

  79. sheepcote Pope | sheep-coat
Ff.
  94. feeder Ff | factor Walker conj.

  76. recks : cares.   So in *Troilus and Cressida*, V, vi, 26.   Cf. *Hamlet*, I, iii, 51 ; *Two Gentlemen of Verona*, IV, iii, 40.

  78. cote : cottage.   This form is usual in compound words.

  82. As far as my voice has the power to bid you welcome.   " So far as I have authority to bid you welcome." — Clar.

  86. stand with : be consistent with.   Cf. *Coriolanus*, II, iii, 9.

  90. waste : spend.   So in *The Merchant of Venice*, III, iv, 12.

  94. feeder : servant, shepherd.   Walker's suggestion that 'factor' (in the sense of 'business agent') was a fitter word here than 'feeder' was adopted in previous editions of Hudson's Shakespeare.

Scene V. *The forest*

Enter Amiens, Jaques, *and others*

Song

AMIENS.　　　Under the greenwood tree
　　　　　　　Who loves to lie with me,
　　　　　　　And turn his merry note
　　　　　　　Unto the sweet bird's throat,
　　Come hither, come hither, come hither:　　　　5
　　　　　　　Here shall he see
　　　　　　　No enemy
　　　　　But winter and rough weather.

JAQUES. More, more, I prithee, more.　　　　9

AMIENS. It will make you melancholy, Monsieur Jaques.

JAQUES. I thank it. More, I prithee, more. I can suck melancholy out of a song, as a weasel sucks eggs. More, I prithee, more.

AMIENS. My voice is ragged: I know I cannot please you.　　　　15

JAQUES. I do not desire you to please me; I do desire you to sing. Come, more; another stanzo: call you 'em stanzos?　　　　18

AMIENS. What you will, Monsieur Jaques.

---

1. AMIENS Capell | Ff omit.
3. turn F_3F_4 | turne F_1F_2 | tune Rowe Capell.

6-7. Printed as one line in Ff.
11-13. Printed as verse in Ff.
16-18. Printed as verse in Ff.

1-4. In his study of Lyly, Professor Baker indicates the resemblance in Pandora's speech, *The Woman in the Moon*, III, ii:

　　Wilt thou for my sake go into yon grove,
　　And we will sing unto the wild bird's note?

17. **stanzo**: stanza. In Cotgrave under 'stance' is "also a stanzo, or staffe of verses." Sherwood (1632) adds "a stanzo (of eight verses)."

JAQUES. Nay, I care not for their names; they owe me
nothing. Will you sing?   21

AMIENS. More at your request than to please myself.

JAQUES. Well then, if ever I thank any man, I 'll thank
you; but that they call compliment is like the encounter
of two dog-apes; and when a man thanks me heartily,
methinks I have given him a penny, and he renders me
the beggarly thanks. Come, sing; and you that will not,
hold your tongues.   28

AMIENS. Well, I 'll end the song. — Sirs, cover the while;
the Duke will drink under this tree. — He hath been all
this day to look you.   31

JAQUES. And I have been all this day to avoid him. He
is too disputable for my company: I think of as many
matters as he; but I give heaven thanks, and make no
boast of them. Come, warble, come.   35

SONG

Who doth ambition shun,   [*All together here*]
And loves to live i' the sun,

20. owe F₁ | owne F₂.   24. compliment Pope | complement Ff.

20–21. **they owe me nothing.** In Latin *nomina facere* means to 'enter
an account,' because not only the sums but the names of the parties
are entered. Cicero uses *nomina facere*, 'to lend money,' and *nomen
solvere*, 'to pay a debt'; and in Livy we have *nomen transcribere in
alium*, 'to transfer a debt to another.'

29. **cover**: lay the cloth. This refers to the forthcoming banquet
and is an order for setting out and preparing the table. Accordingly,
at the close of the scene, we have "his banquet is prepar'd."

31. **look you.** Shakespeare repeatedly uses 'look' thus as a transi-
tive verb. Cf. *The Merry Wives of Windsor*, IV, ii, 83; *Henry V*,
IV, vii, 76. See Abbott, § 200.

33. **disputable**: disputatious. See Abbott, § 3.

> Seeking the food he eats,
> And pleas'd with what he gets,
> Come hither, come hither, come hither: 40
> Here shall he see
> No enemy
> But winter and rough weather.

JAQUES. I 'll give you a verse to this note, that I made
yesterday in despite of my invention.   45

AMIENS. And I 'll sing it.

JAQUES. Thus it goes: —

> If it do come to pass
> That any man turn ass,
> Leaving his wealth and ease   50
> A stubborn will to please,
> Ducdame, ducdame, ducdame:
> Here shall he see
> Gross fools as he,
> And if he will come to me.   55

---

44. JAQUES | Amy (Amiens) F1.   52. Ducdame Ff | Duc ad me Hanmer.

45. **in despite of my invention**: in despite of my lack of imagination. Such elliptical expressions àre not uncommon in Shakespeare.
So in III, ii, 27–28, " He that hath learn'd no wit by nature nor art
may complain of good breeding" evidently means ' may complain of,'
' may complain of want of.' See note, p. 67, l. 28.

52. Furness draws attention to the fact that this phrase has been
proved, " satisfactorily to the provers, to be not only Latin, but Italian, and French, and Gaelic, and Welsh, and Greek !" Hanmer's
suggestion that the reading should be *duc ad me*, ' bring him to me,'
was adopted in previous editions of Hudson's Shakespeare; but it
is probable that W. Aldis Wright is near the truth when he says:
" It is in vain that any meaning is sought for this jargon, as Jaques
only intended to fill up a line with sounds that have no sense."
Canon Ainger suggested a change to ' duc-do′-me ' for the sake of
rhyming with the last verse of the parody, "And if he will come to me."

AMIENS. What's that 'ducdame'?

JAQUES. 'T is a Greek invocation, to call fools into a
circle. I'll go sleep, if I can; if I cannot, I'll rail against
all the first-born of Egypt.   59

AMIENS. And I'll go seek the Duke: his banquet is
prepar'd.   [*Exeunt severally*]

SCENE VI. *The forest*

Enter ORLANDO *and* ADAM

ADAM. Dear master, I can go no further: O, I die for
food! Here lie I down, and measure out my grave. Farewell, kind master.   3

ORLANDO. Why, how now, Adam! no greater heart in
thee? Live a little; comfort a little; cheer thyself a little.
If this uncouth forest yield any thing savage, I will either
be food for it, or bring it for food to thee. Thy conceit
is nearer death than thy powers. For my sake be comfortable; hold death awhile at the arm's end: I will here be
with thee presently; and if I bring thee not something to

---

61. [*Exeunt severally*] Theobald
| Exeunt Ff.

1-16. Printed as verse in Ff.
First as prose by Pope.

57. This account of 'ducdame,' read in the light of the speaker's
character, should go far to prove the theory of W. Aldis Wright.
'To call fools into a circle' is cynically prescient of what the
expression has actually done.

59. the first-born of Egypt. Probably, as Johnson suggested, a
proverbial expression for highborn persons. See *Exodus*, xi, 5.

1. die for: die for lack of. Cf. II, iv, 70; III, ii, 28.

5. comfort: fortify thyself. See Century. Cf. 'comfortable,' ll. 8, 9.

6. uncouth: unknown. — savage: wild.

7. conceit: imagination. So in *Hamlet*, III, iv, 114.

eat, I will give thee leave to die : but if thou diest before
I come, thou art a mocker of my labour. Well said ! thou
look'st cheerly ; and I 'll be with thee quickly. Yet thou
liest in the bleak air : come, I will bear thee to some shel-
ter ; and thou shalt not die for lack of a dinner, if there
live any thing in this desert. Cheerly, good Adam !   16

[Exeunt]

SCENE VII. *The forest*

A table set out. Enter DUKE SENIOR, AMIENS, *and* Lords
like outlaws

DUKE SENIOR. I think he be transform'd into a beast ;
For I can no where find him like a man.

FIRST LORD. My lord, he is but even now gone hence :
Here was he merry, hearing of a song.

· DUKE SENIOR. If he, compact of jars, grow musical,   5
We shall have shortly discord in the spheres.
Go, seek him ; tell him I would speak with him.

Enter JAQUES

FIRST LORD. He saves my labour by his own approach.

DUKE SENIOR. Why, how now, monsieur ! what a life is
        this,
That your poor friends must woo your company !   10
What, you look merrily !

12. **said** : done. So in *1 Henry IV*, V, iv, 75 : " Well said, Hal."
5. **compact of jars** : composed of discords. A pun upon ' jars.'
6. If things are going so contrary to their natural order, the music
of the spheres will soon be untuned. Cf. *Twelfth Night*, III, i, 121.

JAQUES. A fool, a fool ! — I met a fool i' the forest,
A motley fool ; — a miserable world ! —
As I do live by food, I met a fool ;
Who laid him down and bask'd him in the sun,   15
And rail'd on Lady Fortune in good terms,
In good set terms, and yet a motley fool.
'Good morrow, fool,' quoth I.   'No, sir,' quoth he,
'Call me not fool till heaven hath sent me fortune' :
And then he drew a dial from his poke,   20
And, looking on it with lack-lustre eye,
Says very wisely, 'It is ten o'clock :
Thus we may see,' quoth he, 'how the world wags :
'T is but an hour ago since it was nine ;
And after one hour more 't will be eleven ;   25
And so, from hour to hour, we ripe and ripe,
And then, from hour to hour, we rot and rot ;
And thereby hangs a tale.' When I did hear
The motley fool thus moral on the time,
My lungs began to crow like chanticleer,   30
That fools should be so deep-contemplative ;

13. **A motley fool.** So called because the professional fool wore a
patchwork or parti-colored dress. The old sense of 'motley' still
lives in 'mottled.' See Skeat.

19. It will be time enough to call me fool when I shall have got
rich. So in Ray's *Collection of English Proverbs :* "Fortune favours
fools, or fools have the best luck." So, too, Ben Jonson, in the opening lines of the Prologue to *The Alchemist :*

> Fortune, that favours fools, these two short hours
> We wish away, both for your sakes and ours.

20. **dial :** pocket dial, watch. — **poke :** wallet. Hence 'pocket.'
29. **moral :** moralize. But Schmidt says it is probably an adjective,
a view strengthened, according to Furness, by the preposition 'on.'

And I did laugh sans intermission
An hour by his dial. — O noble fool !
A worthy fool ! Motley 's the only wear.

DUKE SENIOR. What fool is this?   35

JAQUES. O worthy fool ! One that hath been a courtier ;
And says, if ladies be but young and fair,
They have the gift to know it ; and in his brain,
Which is as dry as the remainder biscuit
After a voyage, he hath strange places cramm'd   40
With observation, the which he vents
In mangled forms. — O that I were a fool !
I am ambitious for a motley coat.

DUKE SENIOR. Thou shalt have one.

JAQUES.   It is my only suit ;
Provided that you weed your better judgments   45

32. **sans.** " The French preposition *sans* (from Lat. *sine*, as 'certes'
from *certe*) was actually adopted for a time as an English word." —
Clar. So in l. 165 ; *The Tempest*, I, ii, 97 ; *Othello*, I, iii, 64, etc.

39. So Ben Jonson, in the Introduction to *Every Man Out of His
Humour* :

> And, now and then, breaks a dry biscuit jest,
> Which, that it may more easily be chewed,
> He steeps in his own laughter.

And in *Batman uppon Bartholeme*, quoted by W. Aldis Wright, we
have : " Good desposition of the braine and euill is knowne by his
deedes, for if the substaunce of the braine be soft, thinne, and cleere :
it receiueth lightly the feeling & printing of shapes, and lykenesses
of thinges. He that hath such a braine is swift, and good of perseuer-
ance and teaching. When it is contrarye, the braine is not softe :
eyther if he be troubled, he that hath such a braine receiueth slowly
the feeling and printing of thinges : But neuerthelesse when hee hath
taken and receiued them, he keepeth them long in minde. And that
is signe and token of drinesse." Cf. *Troilus and Cressida*, I, iii, 329.

44. **suit.** This pun is repeated in IV, i, 80.

Of all opinion that grows rank in them
That I am wise. I must have liberty
Withal, as large a charter as the wind,
To blow on whom I please ; for so fools have ;
And they that are most galled with my folly,   50
They most must laugh. And why, sir, must they so?
The ' why ' is plain as way to parish church :
He that a fool doth very wisely hit
Doth very foolishly, although he smart,
Seem senseless of the bob: if not,   55
The wise man's folly is anatomized
Even by the squandering glances of the fool.
Invest me in my motley ; give me leave
To speak my mind, and I will through and through
Cleanse the foul body of the infected world,   60
If they will patiently receive my medicine.

    DUKE SENIOR. Fie on thee ! I can tell what thou wouldst do.

    JAQUES. What, for a counter, would I do but good?

    DUKE SENIOR. Most mischievous foul sin, in chiding sin :
For thou thyself hast been a libertine,   65

---

55. **Seem senseless** Ff | Not to   to seem senseless Collier Dyce.
seem senseless Theobald Camb | But   56. **wise man's** | Wise-man's F1.

48–49. " The wind bloweth where it listeth." Cf. *Henry V*, I, i, 48.
   55. To complete the sense and the metre Theobald added ' Not
to ' to the beginning of the line. Ingleby and Furness sustain the
Folio reading. The meaning is : He who feels himself hit must seem
not to feel it ; and if he does not so seem, he simply exposes himself. — **senseless of**: insensible to. — **bob**: rap, taunt. See Murray.
   57. **squandering glances**: random thrusts.
   63. A ' counter ' was a small disk of metal, of little value, used in
making calculations. So in *The Winter's Tale*, IV, iii, 38 : " What
comes the wool to ? . . . I cannot do 't without counters."

As sensual as the brutish sting itself;
And all the embossed sores and headed evils,
That thou with license of free foot hast caught,
Wouldst thou disgorge into the general world.

JAQUES. Why, who cries out on pride,   70
That can therein tax any private party?
Doth it not flow as hugely as the sea,
Till that the weary very means do ebb?
What woman in the city do I name,
When that I say, the city-woman bears   75
The cost of princes on unworthy shoulders?
Who can come in and say that I mean her,
When such a one as she such is her neighbour?
Or what is he of basest function,
That says his bravery is not on my cost,   80
Thinking that I mean him, but therein suits
His folly to the mettle of my speech?
There then; how then? what then? Let me see wherein
My tongue hath wrong'd him: if it do him right,
Then he hath wrong'd himself; if he be free,   85

---

73. **weary very means** F₄ Camb | very means Singer Wright | very very
wearie verie meanes F₁F₂ | wearer's   means Pope.

67. **embossed**: protuberant. Cf. *King Lear*, II, iv, 227. — **headed**:
come to a head. Cf. *Richard II*, V, i, 58.

71. **tax** · accuse. So in l. 86. See note on 'taxation,' p. 15, l. 75.

73. In previous editions of Hudson's Shakespeare, Singer's emendation 'wearer's' for the 'wearie' of First Folio was adopted.
'Wearer's' seems appropriate, as Jaques is referring to the pride of
dress, but the original text is intelligible as it stands.

75. **city-woman**: citizen's wife. A case of "aping their betters."

79. **function**: occupation. So in *Measure for Measure*, III, ii, 264.

80. **bravery**: finery. So in *Measure for Measure*, I, iii, 10; *Sonnets*,
XXXIV, 4·

Why, then my taxing like a wild-goose flies,
Unclaim'd of any man. — But who comes here?

Enter ORLANDO, *with his sword drawn*

ORLANDO. Forbear, and eat no more !
JAQUES.   Why, I have eat none yet.
ORLANDO. Nor shalt not, till necessity be served.
JAQUES. Of what kind should this cock come of?   90
DUKE SENIOR. Art thou thus bolden'd, man, by thy distress,
Or else a rude despiser of good manners,
That in civility thou seem'st so empty?
ORLANDO. You touch'd my vein at first : the thorny point
Of bare distress hath ta'en me from the show   95
Of smooth civility : yet am I inland bred,
And know some nurture. But forbear, I say :

87. comes F₂ | come F₁. — Scene   *Enter . . .* | Enter Orlando Ff.
VIII Pope.   95. hath F₁ | that hath F₂F₃F₄.

90. For other examples of this doubling of the preposition, a common Elizabethan usage, see l. 138 of this scene. — should. Shakespeare often has 'should' in questions where 'can' or 'is' would be used to-day.

93. civility: courtesy. So in *The Merchant of Venice*, II, ii, 204.

94. vein: humor. So in *A Midsummer Night's Dream*, III, ii, 82.

96. inland bred. 'Inland' is often opposed to 'upland,' which in Middle English (as in modern Scotch) is often used in the sense of 'rustic,' 'uncivilized,' as in Henryson's *The Uplandis Mous and the Burges Mous*, or Sir David Lyndsay's

> Then sall I swear I made it but in mowes,
> For upland lassies that keep kye and yowes.

Shakespeare's use of 'inland' (cf. III, ii, 325) may have grown from the fact that up to the Elizabethan time all the mainsprings of culture in England were literally inland, remote from the sea.

97. nurture: education, good breeding. Cf. *The Tempest*, IV, i, 189.

He dies that touches any of this fruit
Till I and my affairs are answered.

    JAQUES. And you will not be answer'd with reason, I
        must die.   100

    DUKE SENIOR. What would you have? Your gentleness
        shall force,
More than your force move us to gentleness.

    ORLANDO. I almost die for food ; and let me have it.

    DUKE SENIOR. Sit down and feed, and welcome to our table.

    ORLANDO. Speak you so gently? Pardon me, I pray you :
I thought that all things had been savage here ;   106
And therefore put I on the countenance
Of stern commandment. But whate'er you are,
That in this desert inaccessible,
Under the shade of melancholy boughs,   . 110
Lose and neglect the creeping hours of time ;
If ever you have look'd on better days,
If ever been where bells have knoll'd to church,
If ever sat at any good man's feast,
If ever from your eyelids wip'd a tear,   115
And know what 't is to pity and be pitied,
Let gentleness my strong enforcement be :
In the which hope I blush, and hide my sword.

    DUKE SENIOR. True is it that we have seen better days,
And have with holy bell been knoll'd to church,   120
And sat at good men's feasts, and wip'd our eyes
Of drops that sacred pity hath engender'd :
And therefore sit you down in gentleness,

---

100. And Ff | An Capell | If Pope.   111. Lose F4 | Loose F1F2F3.

100. And: if. For 'and' in this sense, see Murray, and Abbott, § 101.

And take upon command what help we have
That to your wanting may be minister'd.   125

ORLANDO. Then but forbear your food a little while,
Whiles, like a doe, I go to find my fawn
And give it food. There is an old poor man,
Who after me hath many a weary step
Limp'd in pure love : till he be first suffic'd,   130
Oppress'd with two weak evils, age and hunger,
I will not touch a bit.

DUKE SENIOR.   Go find him out,
And we will nothing waste till you return.

ORLANDO. I thank ye ; and be bless'd for your good
        comfort !   [*Exit*]

DUKE SENIOR. Thou see'st we are not all alone unhappy :
This wide and universal theatre   136
Presents more woeful pageants than the scene
Wherein we play in.

JAQUES.   All the world 's a stage,
And all the men and women merely players :
They have their exits and their entrances ;   140
And one man in his time plays many parts,
His acts being seven ages. At first the infant,

---

135. Scene IX Pope.   142. At first Ff | As, first Capell Dyce.

124. **And take upon command.** Take as you may choose to order, at your will and pleasure. In Lodge's *Rosalynde* we have it thus : "Gerismond . . . tooke him by the hand and badde him welcome, willing him to sit downe in his place, and in his roome not onely to eat his fill, but be Lorde of the feast."

138. **All the world 's a stage.** See Introduction, p. xiii.

139. In the First Folio there is a comma after 'women,' which may indicate a significant pause in the original rendering of the line.

142. **His acts being seven ages.** See Introduction, p. xiv.

Mewling and puking in the nurse's arms.
Then the whining schoolboy, with his satchel
And shining morning face, creeping like snail   145
Unwillingly to school. And then the lover,
Sighing like furnace, with a woeful ballad
Made to his mistress' eyebrow. Then a soldier,
Full of strange oaths, and bearded like the pard,
Jealous in honour, sudden and quick in quarrel,   150
Seeking the bubble reputation
Even in the cannon's mouth. And then the justice,
In fair round belly with good capon lin'd,
With eyes severe and beard of formal cut,
Full of wise saws and modern instances;   155
And so he plays his part. The sixth age shifts
Into the lean and slipper'd pantaloon,
With spectacles on nose and pouch on side,
His youthful hose, well sav'd, a world too wide
For his shrunk shank ; and his big manly voice,   160
Turning again toward childish treble, pipes
And whistles in his sound. Last scene of all,
That ends this strange eventful history,
Is second childishness and mere oblivion,
Sans teeth, sans eyes, sans taste, sans every thing.   165

144. Then Ff | And then Rowe.   **148. a soldier** Ff | the soldier Dyce.

149. pard : leopard. In Keats, *Lamia*, is "freckled like a pard."
155. saws : sayings. — **modern instances** : commonplace examples.
For this use of 'modern,' cf. IV, i, 6 ; *Macbeth*, IV, iii, 170 ; *Antony
and Cleopatra*, V, ii, 167.
157. pantaloon. A stereotyped character in the old Italian farces ;
it represented a thin, emaciated, old dotard in slippers.
162. his its. See Abbott, § 228.

Re-enter ORLANDO, *with* ADAM

DUKE SENIOR. Welcome. Set down your venerable burthen,
And let him feed.

ORLANDO. I thank you most for him.

ADAM.   So had you need;
I scarce can speak to thank you for myself.

DUKE SENIOR. Welcome; fall to: I will not trouble you
As yet, to question you about your fortunes. —   171
Give us some music; and, good cousin, sing.

SONG

AMIENS.   Blow, blow, thou winter wind,
              Thou art not so unkind
                 As man's ingratitude;   175
              Thy tooth is not so keen,
              Because thou art not seen,
                 Although thy breath be rude.
        Heigh-ho! sing, heigh-ho! unto the green holly:
        Most friendship is feigning, most loving mere folly: 180
              Then, heigh-ho, the holly!
                 This life is most jolly.

166. Scene X Pope.
174-177. Two lines in Ff.
177. **Because thou art not seen** |
Thou causest not that teen Hanmer

| Because the heart's not seen
Farmer conj. | Because thou art
foreseen Staunton conj.
181. **Then,** Rowe | the Ff.

174. **unkind**: unnatural. So 'unkind daughters' in *King Lear*, III,
iv, 73.

177. In previous editions of Hudson's Shakespeare, Staunton's
conjecture was adopted as an emendation of the Folio text. The
best defense of the Folio text is Harness's note: "I never perceived
any difficulty till it was pointed out by the commentators, but supposed the words to mean that the inclemency of the wind was not so
severely felt as the ingratitude of man, because the foe is unseen,
i.e. unknown, and the sense of injury is not heightened by the
recollection of any former kindness."

> Freeze, freeze, thou bitter sky,
> That dost not bite so nigh
>   As benefits forgot: 185
> Though thou the waters warp,
> Thy sting is not so sharp
>   As friend remember'd not.
>   Heigh-ho! sing, etc.   189

DUKE SENIOR. If that you were the good Sir Rowland's son,
As you have whisper'd faithfully you were,
And as mine eye doth his effigies witness
Most truly limn'd and living in your face,
Be truly welcome hither: I am the Duke
That lov'd your father: the residue of your fortune,   195
Go to my cave and tell me. Good old man,
Thou art right welcome as thy master is.
Support him by the arm. Give me your hand,
And let me all your fortunes understand.   [*Exeunt*]

183-184, 186-187. One line in Ff.   197. **master** | masters F1.

186. **warp.** W. Aldis Wright, holding that in 'warp' there are ety-mologically the two ideas of throwing and turning, says: "We may therefore understand by the warping of the waters, either the change produced in them by the action of the frost, or the bending and ruffling of their surface caused by the wintry wind." But in Elizabethan English the verb 'warp' was often used in the sense of 'weave.' For example, — literally, in Sylvester's Du Bartas's *Battle of Ivry*:

> This Gold-grownd Web to weave, to warp, to spin;

figuratively, in Sternhold's version of the *Psalms*:

> While he doth mischief warp.

The appropriateness of the 'weave' figure may be seen in the fine network appearance which water assumes in the first stages of crys-tallization. Propertius has a line containing a similar figure: *Africus in glaciem frigore nectit aquas.*

187–188. Contrast with this the close of Wordsworth's *Simon Lee.*

ACT III

SCENE I. *A room in the palace*

Enter DUKE FREDERICK, OLIVER, Lords, *and* Attendants

DUKE FREDERICK. Not see him since? Sir, sir, that
    cannot be :
But were I not the better part made mercy,
I should not seek an absent argument
Of my revenge, thou present. But look to it :
Find out thy brother, wheresoe'er he is ;   5
Seek him with candle ; bring him dead or living
Within this twelvemonth, or turn thou no more
To seek a living in our territory.
Thy lands and all things that thou dost call thine
Worth seizure do we seize into our hands,   10
Till thou canst quit thee by thy brother's mouth
Of what we think against thee.

OLIVER. O that your Highness knew my heart in this !
I never lov'd my brother in my life.

DUKE FREDERICK. More villain thou. — Well, push him
    out of doors ;   15
And let my officers of such a nature

3. seek F1 | see F2F3F4.

2. **the better part**: for the greater part. See Abbott, § 202.
3. **argument**: subject. Compare the use of 'argument' in I, ii, 259.
6. **Seek him with candle.** Cf. *Zephaniah*, i, 12 ; *Luke*, xv, 18.
11. **quit**: acquit. So in *Henry V*, II, ii, 166.

Make an extent upon his house and lands :
Do this expediently and turn him going.   [*Exeunt*]

SCENE II. *The forest*

Enter ORLANDO, *with a paper*

ORLANDO. Hang there, my verse, in witness of my love :
   And thou, thrice-crowned queen of night, survey
With thy chaste eye, from thy pale sphere above,
   Thy huntress' name, that my full life doth sway.
O Rosalind ! these trees shall be my books,   5
   And in their barks my thoughts I 'll character ;
That every eye which in this forest looks

17. **extent.** A law phrase, thus explained by Blackstone : " The process hereon is usually called an extent or *extendi facias*, because the Sheriff is to cause the lands, etc., to be appraised to their full extended value, before he delivers them to the plaintiff."

18. **expediently** : expeditiously. So 'expedient' in *Richard II*, I, iv, 39.

2. **thrice-crowned.** Luna, Selene, or Cynthia, in the heavens; Proserpina, Persephone, or Hecate, in the underworld; Diana, or Artemis, on earth — such were the names and realms of the " queen of night," as they are found in classical mythology. Johnson quotes the famous memorial couplet : —

> Terret, lustrat, agit ; Proserpina, Luna, Diana ;
> Ima, superna, feras ; sceptro, fulgore, sagittis.

Cf. Vergil's *Æneid*, IV, 511. In Chapman's *Hymnus in Cynthiam* (*The Shadow of Night*, 1594) occurs the highly poetical passage :

> Nature's bright eye-sight, and the night's fair soul,
> That with thy triple forehead dost control
> Earth, seas, and hell.

Cf. *A Midsummer Night's Dream*, V, i, 391.

6. **character** : write. Writing love-verses on the bark of trees is an old pastoral convention. Cf. Vergil's *Eclogues*, V, 13–14.

Shall see thy virtue witness'd everywhere.

Run, run, Orlando ; carve on every tree   9

The fair, the chaste, and unexpressive she.   [*Exit*]

Enter CORIN *and* TOUCHSTONE

CORIN. And how like you this shepherd's life, Master
Touchstone?   12

TOUCHSTONE. Truly, shepherd, in respect of itself, it is a
good life ; but in respect that it is a shepherd's life, it is
naught. In respect that it is solitary, I like it very well ;
but in respect that it is private, it is a very vile life. Now,
in respect it is in the fields, it pleaseth me well ; but in
respect it is not in the court, it is tedious. As it is a spare
life, look you, it fits my humour well ; but as there is no
more plenty in it, it goes much against my stomach. Hast
any philosophy in thee, shepherd?   21

CORIN. No more but that I know, the more one sickens
the worse at ease he is ; and that he that wants money,

---

11. Scene III Pope.   16. **vile** | vild Ff.

10. **unexpressive** : inexpressible. Milton twice in his earlier poems
uses this word in a similar way — the active form with the passive
sense :

> Harping in loud and solemn quire,
> With unexpressive notes to Heav'n's new-born Heir.
>   *Hymn on the Nativity*, 116.

> And hears the unexpressive nuptial song. *Lycidas*, 176.

10. **she.** In *Sonnets*, CXXX, Shakespeare uses 'she' for 'woman.'
See Abbott, § 224. Cf. *Twelfth Night*, I, v, 259 ; *Cymbeline*, I, iii, 29 ;
The Taming of the Shrew, III, ii, 236. Crashaw, in *Wishes* (*To His
Supposed Mistress*), has

> Whoe'er she be
> That not impossible she
> That shall command my heart and me.

means, and content is without three good friends; that
the property of rain is to wet and fire to burn; that good
pasture makes fat sheep; and that a great cause of the
night is lack of the sun; that he that hath learn'd no wit
by nature nor art may complain of good breeding, or comes
of a very dull kindred.   29

TOUCHSTONE. Such a one is a natural philosopher. Wast
ever in court, shepherd?

CORIN. No, truly.

TOUCHSTONE. Then thou art damn'd.

CORIN. Nay, I hope, —   34

TOUCHSTONE. Truly, thou art damn'd; like an ill-roasted
egg, all on one side.

CORIN. For not being at court? Your reason.   37

TOUCHSTONE. Why, if thou never wast at court, thou
never saw'st good manners; if thou never saw'st good manners, then thy manners must be wicked; and wickedness is
sin, and sin is damnation. Thou art in a parlous state,
shepherd.   42

CORIN. Not a whit, Touchstone: those that are good
manners at the court are as ridiculous in the country as the

43. **Touchstone** Ff | Mr. Touchstone Capell. — are F₁F₂ | have F₃F₄.

28. **may complain of good breeding**: may complain of the lack of
good breeding. Here, as in II, iv, 69; II, v, 45; II, vi, 1, the expression is elliptical. The usage is common in Elizabethan literature.
In Johnson's *The Sad Shepherd*, Lionel says of Amie: "She's sick
of the young shepherd that bekist her"; i.e. 'sick for want of' him.

30. 'Natural' being a common term for a fool, Touchstone in all
probability is punning on the word.

41. 'Parlous' is a dialectic form of 'perilous,' sometimes used with
a dash of humor, as appears to be the case in this instance. "The
spelling represents the pronunciation." — Clar.

behaviour of the country is most mockable at the court. You told me you salute not at the court, but you kiss your hands : that courtesy would be uncleanly, if courtiers were shepherds.   48

TOUCHSTONE. Instance, briefly ; come, instance.

CORIN. Why, we are still handling our ewes ; and their fells, you know, are greasy.   51

TOUCHSTONE. Why, do not your courtier's hands sweat? and is not the grease of a mutton as wholesome as the sweat of a man? Shallow, shallow. A better instance, I say ; come.   55

CORIN. Besides, our hands are hard.

TOUCHSTONE. Your lips will feel them the sooner. Shallow again. A more sounder instance, come.   58

CORIN. And they are often tarr'd over with the surgery of our sheep ; and would you have us kiss tar? The court-ier's hands are perfum'd with civet.   61

TOUCHSTONE. Most shallow man ! thou worms-meat, in respect of a good piece of flesh indeed ! Learn of the wise, and perpend : civet is of a baser birth than tar, the very uncleanly flux of a cat. Mend the instance, shepherd.   65

---

53. a mutton F1 | mutton F3F4.   63. flesh indeed ! | flesh, indeed !
                                                                    Theobald.

46. but you kiss : without kissing. See Abbott, § 118.

51. The original meaning of 'fell' is 'skin' or 'hide of an animal.' Thus the word is used by Chaucer (*Troilus*, I, 91), and thus Shake-speare uses the word in *King Lear*, V, iii. While in *Macbeth*, V, v, 11, we have the expression 'fell of hair,' the Elizabethan usage dis-criminated between 'fleece' and 'fell'; as in Jonson's *Discoveries:* "A prince is the pastor of the people. He ought to shear, not to flea (flay) his sheep; to take their fleeces, not their fells."

58. more sounder. See Abbott, § 11. Pope omitted 'more.'

64. perpend : consider. Cf. *Hamlet*, II, ii, 105.

CORIN. You have too courtly a wit for me : I 'll rest.

TOUCHSTONE. Wilt thou rest damn'd? God help thee, shallow man ! God make incision in thee ! thou art raw. 68

CORIN. Sir, I am a true labourer: I earn that I eat, get that I wear, owe no man hate, envy no man's happiness, glad of other men's good, content with my harm ; and the greatest of my pride is, to see my ewes graze and my lambs suck.   73

TOUCHSTONE. That is another simple sin in you, to bring the ewes and the rams together. If thou be'st not damn'd for this, the devil himself will have no shepherds ; I cannot see else how thou shouldst 'scape.   77

CORIN. Here comes young Master Ganymede, my new mistress's brother.

Enter ROSALIND, *reading a paper*

ROSALIND. From the east to western Ind,   80
           No jewel is like Rosalind.
           Her worth, being mounted on the wind,
           Through all the world bears Rosalind.

77. else | F₃F₄ omit.   80. . . . *reading a paper* Capell
78. young | F₃F₄ omit — Master | Ff omit. — Scene IV Pope.
| Mr. Ff.

68. The allusion is, apparently, to the practice of surgeons who used cuttings and burnings for the healing of a disease called 'the simples'; a quibble being implied withal between 'simples' and 'simpleton.' His being 'raw' is the reason in Touchstone's logic why incision should be made. Bear in mind that 'raw' is used in the double sense of 'green' and 'sore,' and perhaps this will render the passage clear enough. In this connection it may be interesting to recall Sydney Smith's remark about the necessity of a surgical operation before a joke can be got into the heads of some people !

All the pictures fairest lin'd
Are but black to Rosalind.   85
Let no face be kept in mind
But the fair of Rosalind.

TOUCHSTONE. I 'll rhyme you so eight years together, dinners and suppers and sleeping-hours excepted : it is the right butter-women's rank to market.   90

ROSALIND. Out, fool !

TOUCHSTONE. For a taste :

If a hart do lack a hind,
Let him seek out Rosalind.
If the cat will after kind,   95
So be sure will Rosalind.

---

84. lin'd | Linde   F₁F₂F₃ | Lind F₄ | lin'd Pope | limn'd Capell.
87. the fair of F₁F₂ | the most   fair F₃F₄ | the face of Rowe.
90. rank to F₃F₄ | ranke to F₁F₂ | rate to Hanmer (see below).

84. lin'd : drawn. " That is, most fairly delineated." — Steevens.
87. fair : beauty. So in *Sonnets*, XVI, 11 ; LXXXIII, 2.
90. rank to. For this, the Folio reading, Crosby's conjecture, ' rack to,' was substituted in previous editions of Hudson's Shakespeare. W. Aldis Wright thinks ' rack ' the proper word, and justifies the conjecture by a quotation from Cotgrave, in which ' rack ' is used as synonymous with ' amble.' But if ' rank ' is taken in the sense of ' row ' (cf. ' rank of osiers,' IV, iii, 79), there is no reason why the Folio reading should not be retained. The meaning of the expression would thus be, The lines follow one after another, like butter-women in a row jog-trotting to market. The habit of nicknaming popular verse forms was common in Elizabethan literary coteries. For example, the name ' Poulter's measure ' was given to alternating Alexandrines and septenaries : " The commonest sort of verse which we use now adayes I know not certainly howe to name it, unless I should say that it doth consist of Poulters measure, which giveth xii. for one dozen and xiiii. for another." — Gascoigne, *Notes of Instruction*, 1575.

Winter garments must be lined,
So must slender Rosalind.
They that reap must sheaf and bind;
Then to cart with Rosalind.   100
Sweetest nut hath sourest rind,
Such a nut is Rosalind.
He that sweetest rose will find
Must find love's prick and Rosalind.   104

This is the very false gallop of verses : why do you infect yourself with them?

ROSALIND.   Peace, you dull fool! I found them on a tree.

TOUCHSTONE.   Truly, the tree yields bad fruit.   108

ROSALIND.   I 'll graff it with you, and then I shall graff it with a medlar : then it will be the earliest fruit i' the country ; for you 'll be rotten ere you be half ripe, and that 's the right virtue of the medlar.   112

TOUCHSTONE.   You have said ; but whether wisely or no, let the forest judge.

97. **Winter** F₃F₄ | Wintred F₁F₂.   101. **nut** F₁F₂ | meat F₃F₄.

105. **false gallop.** This expression is still used in certain districts to describe the action of a horse which in galloping lifts the wrong foot first. Malone quotes Nash's *Apologie of Pierce Pennilesse* (1593): " I would trot a false gallop through the rest of his ragged Verses, but that, if I should retort his rime dogrell aright, I must make my verses (as he doth his) run hobling, like a Brewer's Cart upon the stones, and observe no length in their feet."

109. **graff.** The form 'graft' is a corruption of 'graffed.'

110. The medlar is one of the latest fruits, being uneatable till it has grown soft or mellow.   Moreover, though the latest of fruits to ripen, it is one of the earliest to rot.   Does Rosalind mean that when the tree is graffed with Touchstone, its fruit will rot earlier than ever? The obvious pun on 'meddler' is found also in *Timon of Athens*, IV, iii, 305–309.

Enter CELIA, *reading a paper*

ROSALIND. Peace !   115
Here comes my sister, reading : stand aside.
    CELIA. [*Reads*]

        Why should this desert be ?
            For it is unpeopled ? No ;
        Tongues I 'll hang on every tree,
            That shall civil sayings show :   120
        Some, how brief the life of man
            Runs his erring pilgrimage,
        That the stretching of a span
            Buckles in his sum of age ;
        Some, of violated vows   125
            'Twixt the souls of friend and friend :
        But upon the fairest boughs,
            Or at every sentence end,
        Will I Rosalinda write ;
            Teaching all that read to know   130
        The quintessence of every sprite
            Heaven would in little show.

115. Scene V Pope.   a desert be? Rowe.
117. desert be ? | Desert bee, F₁ | 131. The F₁F₂ | This F₃F₄.

118. For: because. So in *The Merchant of Venice*, I, iii, 43. ' For ' in
this sense is an elliptical form of ' for the reason that.' Hence ' for that.'
120. civil sayings : sayings of civilized life. ' Civil ' may here be
used as when we say ' civil ' wisdom and ' civil ' life, in opposition
to a solitary state. Or it may mean ' grave,' ' solemn.'
122. erring · wandering. Not in a moral sense here.
128. sentence end. See Abbott, § 217.
131. quintessence. The fifth essence (*quinta essentia*) of the Pythag-
oreans and mediæval alchemists was above the four terrestrial
elements, or essences, of earth, water, fire, and air, and was the
spirit or soul of the material world.
132. in little : in miniature. Dr. Furness suggests ' the microcosm.'

    Therefore Heaven Nature charg'd
      That one body should be fill'd
    With all graces wide-enlarg'd: 135
      Nature presently distill'd
    Helen's cheek, but not her heart,
      Cleopatra's majesty,
    Atalanta's better part,
      Sad Lucretia's modesty.   140
    Thus Rosalind of many parts
      By heavenly synod was devis'd;
    Of many faces, eyes, and hearts,
      To have the touches dearest priz'd.
    Heaven would that she these gifts should have, 145
    And I to live and die her slave.

ROSALIND. O most gentle Jupiter! what tedious homily
of love have you wearied your parishioners withal, and never
cried, 'Have patience, good people!'   149

---

   133. charg'd F_1 | chang'd F_3F_4.   147. Jupiter Ff | pulpiter Sped-
   137. cheek | cheeke F_1F_2 | cheeks   ding Camb Globe.
F_3F_4.

   139. Atalanta's better part. Commentators have been a good deal
puzzled to make out what this better part really was. It must have
been that wherein Atalanta surpassed the other ladies mentioned.
Her distinction is athletic prowess and nimbleness of foot (l. 263).
A maiden huntress, she took a leading part in the Calydonian boar
hunt. Beset by suitors, she offered herself in marriage to the man
who should outrun her. This would infer exquisite symmetry and
proportion of form; and Orlando must of course imagine all physical
as well as all mental and moral graces, in his 'heavenly Rosalind.'

   147. Jupiter. Few textual variants have been more widely accepted
by editors, conservative and radical alike, than Spedding's substitution of 'pulpiter' here. The Folio reading is defended by Dr.
Furness in this spirited note:

   Spedding's emendation, 'pulpiter,' adopted by the Cambridge editor
and by Dyce in his second edition, but abandoned in his third, is plausible

CELIA. How now! back, friends! — Shepherd, go off a
little. — Go with him, sirrah.   151

TOUCHSTONE. Come, shepherd, let us make an honourable
retreat; though not with bag and baggage, yet with scrip
and scrippage.   [*Exeunt* CORIN *and* TOUCHSTONE]

CELIA. Didst thou hear these verses?   155

ROSALIND. O, yes, I heard them all, and more too; for
some of them had in them more feet than the verses would
bear.   158

CELIA. That's no matter : the feet might bear the verses.

ROSALIND. Ay, but the feet were lame and could not bear
themselves without the verse, and therefore stood lamely in
the verse.   162

CELIA. But didst thou hear without wondering how thy
name should be hang'd and carv'd upon these trees?

---

150. back, friends! | backe friends Ff.   155. Scene VI Pope.

and alluring. It is the word of all words to introduce the train of thought
that follows, with which 'Jupiter' has no connection. This addition of an -*er*
to a noun in order to change it to an agent, like 'moraler' in *Othello*,
'justicer' in *King Lear*, etc., is, as we all know, thoroughly Shakespearian.
Moreover, 'Jupiter' is not printed in italics as though it were a proper name,
to which Wright calls attention, and as it is printed in the only other place
where it is used in this play, II, iv, 1 ; which adds to the likelihood that it
is here a misprint. All these considerations are clamorous for Spedding's
'pulpiter.' But, on the other hand, the text is clear without it; once before
Rosalind has appealed to 'Jupiter,' and to use this mouth-filling oath, which
is 'not dangerous,' may have been one of her characteristics, as certainly
the use of expletives in general is. Although 'Jupiter' is not elsewhere
printed in Roman, yet 'Jove' is, and in this very scene, l. 223; and so also
is 'Judas,' in III, iv, 8. 'Pulpiter' can hardly be called an emendation;
there is no obscurity which amounts to a defect. It is an improvement; and
against verbal improvements, which it is far from impossible to make in
Shakespeare's text, we should, I think, acquire and maintain a dogged habit
of shutting our eyes and closing our ears.

164. should be : was said to be. "'Should' is frequently used in
giving a reported speech." — Clar. See Abbott, § 328.

ROSALIND. I was seven of the nine days out of the wonder
before you came ; for look here what I found on a palm-tree :
I was never so berhym'd since Pythagoras' time, that I was
an Irish rat, which I can hardly remember.   168

CELIA. Trow you who hath done this ?

ROSALIND. Is it a man ?

CELIA. And a chain, that you once wore, about his neck.
Change you colour?   172

ROSALIND. I prithee, who?

CELIA. O Lord, Lord ! it is a hard matter for friends to
meet; but mountains may be remov'd with earthquakes
and so encounter.   176

ROSALIND. Nay, but who is it?

CELIA. Is it possible?

ROSALIND. Nay, I prithee now with most petitionary
vehemence, tell me who it is.   180

---

165. **of the wonder** F1 | of wonder
F2F3F4.

169. **Trow** | Tro Ff.
172. **you** F1F2 | your F3F4.

165. A reference to the "nine days' wonder" proverb.

167. In *The Merchant of Venice*, IV, i, 131, and *Twelfth Night*,
IV, ii, 54-60, we have other references to the doctrine of the trans-
migration of souls as taught by Pythagoras.

168. **an Irish rat.** This romantic way of killing rats in Ireland is
mentioned by Sidney, Jonson, and other Elizabethan writers. So in
The Poetaster (*To the Reader*):

> Rhime them to death, as they do Irish rats
> In drumming tunes.

174. There is a well-known proverb, "Friends may meet, but
mountains never greet." In Holland's translation of Pliny's *Natural
History*, a book much in vogue in Elizabethan England, occurs the
following passage: ". . . Two hilles encountred together, charging
as it were and with violence assaulting one another, yea and retiring
againe with a most mightie noise."

CELIA. O wonderful, wonderful, and most wonderful wonderful ! and yet again wonderful, and after that, out of all
hooping !   183

ROSALIND. Good my complexion ! dost thou think, though
I am caparison'd like a man, I have a doublet and hose in
my disposition? One inch of delay more is a South-sea of
discovery : I prithee, tell me who is it quickly, and speak
apace. I would thou couldst stammer, that thou mightst
pour this conceal'd man out of thy mouth, as wine comes

183. hooping   F₁F₂F₃ | hoping
F₄ | whooping Theobald.
184. complexion F₄ | complection
F₁F₂F₃.

185. hose F₁ | a hose F₂F₃F₄.
186. a South-sea of Ff | a South-
sea off Theobald | a south-sea-off
Capell.

182–183. out of all hooping (whooping) : beyond all exclamations
of astonishment. 'Out of all cry' and 'beyond all ho' are similar
Elizabethan phrases for the expression of astonishment.

184. Good my complexion : my good complexion ! A humorous
reference to her blushes. In previous editions of Hudson's Shakespeare the First Folio spelling, 'complection,' was retained, and the
word was regarded as synonymous with 'complication,' the phrase
being taken to mean 'my good wrapper-up of mystery,' as Celia has
been taunting Rosalind "with half-told, half-withheld intelligence."
Heath's note on the passage is : " I am inclinable to imagine that
the Poet may possibly have written 'Good my coz perplexer,' that is,
I prithee, my perplexing coz."

186–187. Ingleby's suggestive note on this passage is : "Here we
have a tale of questions falling as thick as hail upon the devoted
Celia. See how many things she is called upon to discover ; and
then say whether she has not incurred a laborious and vexatious
duty by her delay in answering the first question. How plain it is
that her inch of delay has cast her upon a South Sea — a vast and
unexplored ocean — of discovery. The more Celia delays her revela-
tion as to who the man is, the more she will have to reveal about
him. Why? Because Rosalind fills up the delay (increases it, in
fact) with fresh interrogatories, whereby Celia becomes lost in a
South Sea of questions." The 'South-sea' is the Pacific Ocean, discovered by Balboa (not 'stout Cortez,' as Keats has it) in 1513.

out of a narrow-mouth'd bottle, either too much at once, or
none at all. I prithee, take the cork out of thy mouth that
I may drink thy tidings. Is he of God's making? What
manner of man? Is his head worth a hat, or his chin worth
a beard?

CELIA. Nay, he hath but a little beard.   195

ROSALIND. Why, God will send more, if the man will be
thankful : let me stay the growth of his beard, if thou delay
me not the knowledge of his chin.

CELIA. It is young Orlando, that tripp'd up the wrestler's
heels and your heart both in an instant.   200

ROSALIND. Nay, but the devil take mocking : speak, sad
brow and true maid.

CELIA. I' faith, coz, 't is he.

ROSALIND. Orlando?

CELIA. Orlando.   205

ROSALIND. Alas the day ! what shall I do with my
doublet and hose?   What did he when thou saw'st him?
What said he? How look'd he? Wherein went he? What
makes he here? Did he ask for me? Where remains he?
How parted he with thee? and when shalt thou see him
again? Answer me in one word.   211

CELIA. You must borrow me Gargantua's mouth first :
't is a word too great for any mouth of this age's size. To

197. **stay** : wait for. So in *Hamlet*, V, ii, 24, and elsewhere.

201–202. Speak with a serious countenance and as a true maid.

208. **Wherein went he** : how was he dressed? Cf. *Twelfth Night*,
III, iv, 415 ; *Much Ado About Nothing*, V, i, 96.

209. **makes** : does. See note, p. 5, l. 26.

212. Gargantua is the name of a most gigantic giant in Rabelais,
who forks five pilgrims, staves and all, into his mouth in a salad,
and afterwards picks them out from between his teeth.

say ay and no to these particulars is more than to answer
in a catechism.   215

ROSALIND. But doth he know that I am in this forest
and in man's apparel? Looks he as freshly as he did the
day he wrestl'd?   218

CELIA. It is as easy to count atomies as to resolve the
propositions of a lover; but take a taste of my finding him,
and relish it with good observance. I found him under a
tree, like a dropp'd acorn.   222

ROSALIND. It may well be call'd Jove's tree, when it
drops forth such fruit.

CELIA. Give me audience, good madam.

ROSALIND. Proceed.   226

CELIA. There lay he, stretch'd along, like a wounded
knight.

ROSALIND. Though it be pity to see such a sight, it well
becomes the ground.   230

CELIA. Cry 'holla' to thy tongue, I prithee; it curvets
unseasonably. He was furnish'd like a hunter.

ROSALIND. O, ominous! he comes to kill my heart.

219. **atomies** F_1F_2 | atomes F_3F_4.
224. **drops forth such** $F_2F_3F_4$ | droppes forth F_1 | drops such Capell.
231. **thy tongue** Rowe | the tongue Ff.
233. **heart** Rowe | hart Ff.

219. **atomies.** "An atomie is a mote flying in the sunne. Any thing so small that it cannot be made lesse."— Bullokar's *English Expositor*, 1616. — **resolve** : solve, answer.

223. The oak was sacred to Jupiter. Cf. *3 Henry VI*, V, ii, 14. See Vergil, *Georgics*, III, 332; *Æneid*, III, 680.

231. 'holla.' This was a term by which the rider restrained and stopped his horse. So in *Venus and Adonis*, 284.

233. A quibble between 'hart' and 'heart.' Cf. *Julius Cæsar*, III, i, 207–208; *Twelfth Night*, IV, i, 63; *Venus and Adonis*, 502, and elsewhere.

CELIA. I would sing my song without a burthen: thou bring'st me out of tune. 235

ROSALIND. Do you not know I am a woman? when I think, I must speak. Sweet, say on.

CELIA. You bring me out. — Soft! comes he not here?

Enter ORLANDO *and* JAQUES

ROSALIND. 'T is he: slink by, and note him. 239

JAQUES. I thank you for your company; but, good faith, I had as lief have been myself alone.

ORLANDO. And so had I; but yet, for fashion sake, I thank you too for your society. 243

JAQUES. God be wi' you! let 's meet as little as we can.

ORLANDO. I do desire we may be better strangers.

JAQUES. I pray you, mar no more trees with writing love-songs in their barks. 247

ORLANDO. I pray you, mar no moe of my verses with reading them ill-favouredly.

238. here | heere F1 | neere F2 | near F3F4.
Enter . . . in Ff after l. 237.

239. Scene VII Pope.
244. be wi' you | buy you Ff.

238. **bring me out**: put me out. Cf. *Love's Labour's Lost*, V, ii, 171.

241. **myself alone**: alone by myself. See Abbott, § 20.

244. **God be wi' you**. Here the Folios have "God buy you." Also in IV, i, 28, of this play: "Nay, then, God buy you, an you talk in blank verse." And in V, iii, 39: "God buy you; and God mend your voices." Of course it is the old contraction of "God be with you," which has been still further shortened into 'good by.'

248. **moe**. This is the reading of the First Folio. In Middle and Elizabethan English the forms 'more' (l. 246) and 'moe' are both found, and, in use, correspond in a general way to *mára* (comparative of *micel*, 'great') and *má* in Anglo-Saxon. "The distinction appears to be that 'moe' is used only with the plural, 'more' both with singular and plural." — Clar.

JAQUES. Rosalind is your love's name?   250
ORLANDO. Yes, just.

JAQUES. I do not like her name.

ORLANDO. There was no thought of pleasing you when she was christen'd.

JAQUES. What stature is she of?   255
ORLANDO. Just as high as my heart.

JAQUES. You are full of pretty answers. Have you not been acquainted with goldsmiths' wives, and conn'd them out of rings?   259

ORLANDO. Not so; but I answer you right painted cloth, from whence you have studied your questions.   261

JAQUES. You have a nimble wit: I think 't was made of Atalanta's heels. Will you sit down with me? and we two will rail against our mistress the world and all our misery.

ORLANDO. I will chide no breather in the world but myself, against whom I know most faults.   266

JAQUES. The worst fault you have is to be in love.

ORLANDO. 'T is a fault I will not change for your best virtue. I am weary of you.   269

---

261. your F₁ | you F₂.   266. most F₁ | no F₂F₃F₄.

258–259. The meaning is, that goldsmiths' wives have given him the freedom of their husbands' shops, where he has committed to memory the mottoes inscribed on their rings and other jewels.

260. answer you right painted cloth: answer you sententiously. 'Painted cloth' was a species of hangings for the walls of rooms, made of canvas painted with various devices and mottoes. The verses, mottoes, and proverbial sentences on such hangings are often made the subject of allusion in old writers. Cf. *Lucrece*, 245; *1 Henry IV*, IV, ii, 28; *Troilus and Cressida*, V, 10, 46.

263. Atalanta's heels. This reference to the nimble-footedness of Atalanta should throw light on the 'better part' of l. 139.

Clímax

JAQUES. By my troth, I was seeking for a fool when I found you.   271

ORLANDO. He is drown'd in the brook : look but in, and you shall see him.

JAQUES. There I shall see mine own figure.   274

ORLANDO. Which I take to be either a fool or a cipher.

JAQUES. I 'll tarry no longer with you : farewell, good Signior Love.   277

ORLANDO. I am glad of your departure : adieu, good Monsieur Melancholy.   [*Exit* JAQUES]

ROSALIND. [*Aside to* CELIA] I will speak to him like a saucy lackey, and under that habit play the knave with him. — Do you hear, forester?   282

ORLANDO. Very well : what would you?

ROSALIND. I pray you, what is 't o'clock?

ORLANDO. You should ask me what time o' day : there 's no clock in the forest.   286

ROSALIND. Then there is no true lover in the forest ; else sighing every minute and groaning every hour would detect the lazy foot of Time as well as a clock.   289

ORLANDO. And why not the swift foot of Time? had not that been as proper?   291

ROSALIND. By no means, sir. Time travels in divers paces with divers persons. I 'll tell you who Time ambles withal, who Time trots withal, who Time gallops withal, and who he stands still withal.   295

ORLANDO. I prithee, who doth he trot withal?

279. [*Exit* . . .] | Ff omit.   296. who F1 | whom F2F3F4 (so
280. Scene VIII Pope.   in ll. 308, 311).

294. **withal**. This is an emphatic form of 'with' used after the object at the end of a sentence. See Abbott, § 196.

ROSALIND. Marry, he trots hard with a young maid between the contract of her marriage and the day it is solemniz'd : if the interim be but a se'nnight, Time's pace is so hard that it seems the length of seven year.   300

ORLANDO. Who ambles Time withal?

ROSALIND. With a priest that lacks Latin, and a rich man that hath not the gout; for the one sleeps easily because he cannot study, and the other lives merrily because he feels no pain; the one lacking the burthen of lean and wasteful learning, the other knowing no burthen of heavy tedious penury : these Time ambles withal.   307

ORLANDO. Who doth he gallop withal?

ROSALIND. With a thief to the gallows ; for, though he go as softly as foot can fall, he thinks himself too soon there.

ORLANDO. Who stays it still withal?   311

ROSALIND. With lawyers in the vacation ; for they sleep between term and term, and then they perceive not how Time moves.

ORLANDO. Where dwell you, pretty youth?   315

ROSALIND. With this shepherdess, my sister; here in the skirts of the forest, like fringe upon a petticoat.

ORLANDO. Are you native of this place?

297–298. Hardly anything is so likely to make a short journey seem long, as riding on a hard-trotting horse, however fast the horse may go. On the other hand, to ride an ambling horse makes a long journey seem short, because the horse rides so easy. It were hardly needful to say this, but that some have lately proposed to invert the order of the nags in this case.

299. se'nnight : a week. That is 'seven-night' (Anglo-Saxon *seofon-niht*). Compare *Much Ado About Nothing*, II, i, 375. This mode of reckoning still survives in 'fortnight,' that is, 'fourteen night.'

318. native. Usually an adjective in Shakespeare.

ROSALIND. As the cony, that you see dwell where she is kindl'd.   320

ORLANDO. Your accent is something finer than you could purchase in so remov'd a dwelling.   322

ROSALIND. I have been told so of many : but indeed an old religious uncle of mine taught me to speak, who was in his youth an inland man ; one that knew courtship too well, for there he fell in love. I have heard him read many lectures against it ; and I thank God I am not a woman, to be touch'd with so many giddy offences as he hath generally tax'd their whole sex withal.   329

ORLANDO. Can you remember any of the principal evils that he laid to the charge of women?   331

ROSALIND. There were none principal : they were all like one another as half-pence are, every one fault seeming monstrous till his fellow-fault came to match it.

ORLANDO. I prithee, recount some of them.   335

ROSALIND. No, I will not cast away my physic but on those that are sick. There is a man haunts the forest, that abuses our young plants with carving Rosalind on their barks ; hangs odes upon hawthorns and elegies on brambles ; all, forsooth, deifying the name of Rosalind : if I

---

327. lectures F_3F_4 | Lectors F_1 | 333. one fault F_1F_2 | ones fault F_3F_4.
Lecturs F_2. — and F_1F_2 | F_3F_4 omit.   340. deifying $F_2F_3F_4$ | defying F_1.

320. **kindl'd** : brought forth. This is the Middle English *kindlen* (Anglo-Saxon *cennan*), 'to produce,' 'to bring forth,' used specially of the littering of rabbits.

322. **purchase** : acquire. — **remov'd** : sequestered.

325. **inland**. See note, p. 58, l. 96. — **courtship**. Rosalind puns upon the word in its double sense of 'court manners' and 'courting.'

328. **touch'd** : tainted. So in *King John*, V, vii, 2.

329. **tax'd** : blamed. See note on 'taxation,' p. 15, l. 75.

could meet that fancy-monger, I would give him some good
counsel, for he seems to have the quotidian of love upon him.

ORLANDO. I am he that is so love-shak'd : I pray you,
tell me your remedy.   344

ROSALIND. There is none of my uncle's marks upon you :
he taught me how to know a man in love; in which cage
of rushes I am sure you are not prisoner.

ORLANDO. What were his marks?   348

ROSALIND. A lean cheek, which you have not; a blue
eye and sunken, which you have not; an unquestionable
spirit, which you have not; a beard neglected, which you
have not; but I pardon you for that, for simply your having
in beard is a younger brother's revenue : then your hose
should be ungarter'd, your bonnet unbanded, your sleeve
unbutton'd, your shoe untied, and every thing about you
demonstrating a careless desolation : but you are no such

347. are | art F1.   353. in beard F1 | no beard F2F3F4.

341. fancy-monger: love-monger. So 'fancy' for 'love' in III, v, 29.

342. quotidian. The name of an intermittent fever, so called because
the fits came on every day. Similarly, 'tertian' and 'quartan' were
applied to those that came on once in three and once in four days.

349-350. a blue eye. With blueness about the eyes, such as to indicate sleeplessness, hunger, dejection. Cf. *Lucrece*, 1587. Interesting
evidence may be gathered from Shakespeare and Elizabethan poetry
generally in support of the contention that what are now known as
'blue' eyes were called 'gray' in the sixteenth century.

350-351. an unquestionable spirit: a reserved, unsociable spirit.
The reverse of that in *Hamlet*, I, iv, 43.

> Thou comest in such a questionable shape
> That I will speak to thee.

352. having: possession. Under the law of primogeniture, a
younger brother's revenue was likely to be small. Orlando is too
young for his possession in way of a beard to amount to much.

man; you are rather point-device in your accoutrements, as loving yourself than seeming the lover of any other.   358

ORLANDO. Fair youth, I would I could make thee believe I love.   360

ROSALIND. Me believe it! you may as soon make her that you love believe it; which, I warrant, she is apter to do than to confess she does: that is one of the points in the which women still give the lie to their consciences. But, in good sooth, are you he that hangs the verses on the trees, wherein Rosalind is so admir'd?   366

ORLANDO. I swear to thee, youth, by the white hand of Rosalind, I am that he, that unfortunate he.

ROSALIND. But are you so much in love as your rhymes speak?   370

ORLANDO. Neither rhyme nor reason can express how much.

ROSALIND. Love is merely a madness; and, I tell you, deserves as well a dark house and a whip as madmen do: and the reason why they are not so punish'd and cured is, that the lunacy is so ordinary that the whippers are in love too. Yet I profess curing it by counsel.   376

ORLANDO. Did you ever cure any so?

ROSALIND. Yes, one, and in this manner. He was to imagine me his love, his mistress; and I set him every day to woo me: at which time would I, being but a moonish youth, grieve, be effeminate, changeable, longing, and lik-ing; proud, fantastical, apish, shallow, inconstant, full of

---

357. rather | rather a F₃F₄. — accoutrements | accoustrements Ff.

357. point-device (Old Fr. *à point devis*): precise. See Skeat.
374. This shows how lunatics were often treated in the sixteenth century. Cf. *Twelfth Night*, III, iv, 148; V, i, 350.
380. moonish: changeable. But Halliwell suggests 'foolish,' 'weak.'

tears, full of smiles; for every passion something, and for no passion truly any thing, as boys and women are for the most part cattle of this colour: would now like him, now loathe him; then entertain him, then forswear him; now weep for him, then spit at him; that I drave my suitor from his mad humour of love to a living humour of madness; which was, to forswear the full stream of the world and to live in a nook merely monastic. And thus I cured him; and this way will I take upon me to wash your liver as clean as a sound sheep's heart, that there shall not be one spot of love in 't.

ORLANDO. I would not be cur'd, youth.   393

ROSALIND. I would cure you, if you would but call me Rosalind, and come every day to my cote and woo me.

ORLANDO. Now, by the faith of my love, I will: tell me where it is.   397

ROSALIND. Go with me to it, and I 'll show it you; and by the way you shall tell me where in the forest you live. Will you go?   400

ORLANDO. With all my heart, good youth.

ROSALIND. Nay, you must call me Rosalind. — Come, sister, will you go?   [*Exeunt*]

387. my F₁F₂F₃ | this F₄. — from F₁F₂F₃ | for F₄.

388. living . . . madness Ff | mad . . . loving Johnson conj.

391. clean | cleane F₁ | cleare F₂ | cleer F₃ | clear F₄.

402. Nay F₁F₂F₃ | Nay, Nay F₄.

388. In the text of previous editions of Hudson's Shakespeare, Johnson's suggested substitution of ' loving ' for ' living ' — the reading of the Folios — was adopted. But if ' living ' be taken in the sense of ' real,' ' active,' the Folio reading may well be retained.

390. **merely**: entirely. So in *The Tempest*, I, i, 59.

391. **liver**. The liver was supposed to be the seat of the passions and affections, especially of love and courage. Shakespeare very often speaks of it so, as in *The Tempest*, IV, i, 56.

SCENE III. *The forest*

Enter TOUCHSTONE *and* AUDREY ; JAQUES *behind*

TOUCHSTONE. Come apace, good Audrey : I will fetch
up your goats, Audrey. And how, Audrey? am I the man
yet? doth my simple feature content you?   3

SCENE III | Scene IX Pope.   2. how F₁F₂ | now F₃F₄.

AUDREY. This is a popular abbreviation or corruption of the
Saxon name Etheldreda. The name 'St. Audrey,' for St. Etheldreda,
is found on old calendars. The adjective 'tawdry' comes from the
phrase 'tawdrie lace,' i.e. 'St. Audrey lace,' a kind of common lace
(some say, necklace) bought at St. Audrey's Fair, held at the shrine
of the saint in the Isle of Ely.

3. feature. This word (Old Fr. *faiture* from Lat. *factura*) means
here either 'personal appearance' (cf. 'make') or 'a literary composition.' In defense of the latter interpretation, Mr. Joseph Crosby
writes :

Mr. W. Wilkins, of Trinity College, Dublin, has recently pointed out that
'feature' formerly meant a literary work, a poem, a drama, etc., just as we
now call such a work 'a composition'; being from the Latin verb *facere*, 'to
make.' Ben Jonson uses the word in this sense when he says of his creation,
the play of *Volpone*, that two months before it was no 'feature':

> To this there needs no lie, but this his creature,
> Which was two months since no feature ;
> And, though he dares give them five lives to mend
> 'T is known, five weeks fully penned it.

Various other examples of the use of this word in the sense of a literary production have been discovered, even as far back as the time of Pliny, who, in
the Preface to his *Natural History*, speaks of his work as *libri nati apud me
proxima fetura*.[1] . . . From the context we find that Touchstone calls himself 'a poet,' and is nettled because his verses "cannot be understood," and
laments that the gods had not made his rustic adorer 'poetical.' Here, instead
of asking, as the question is commonly supposed to signify, " How does my
intelligent countenance strike you now?" it is evident that, being a clown of
brains and observation, he had been making love, as he had seen it done 'at

[1] But *fetura* is etymologically a different word from *factura*.

AUDREY. Your features ! Lord warrant us ! what features?

TOUCHSTONE. I am here with thee and thy goats, as the most capricious poet, honest Ovid, was among the Goths.

JAQUES. [*Aside*] O knowledge ill-inhabited, worse than Jove in a thatch'd house !   8

TOUCHSTONE. When a man's verses cannot be understood, nor a man's good wit seconded with the forward

court,' by sending 'good Audrey' a poetical billet-doux; and his question means, "How are you pleased with my love-ditty?" He tells us elsewhere that he "could rhyme you eight years together, dinners and suppers and sleeping-hours excepted"; and no wonder he felt chagrined that his 'simple feature,' as he modestly terms his love-rhymes, was unregarded, and his 'good wit' thrown away, "not being seconded with the forward child, understanding." It was not his good looks that the clever and sharp-witted fellow was sensitive about: Audrey could have had no trouble to understand them: it was the nonappreciation of his gallant poetical 'feature' that disgusted him, and struck him "more dead than a great reckoning in a little room."

6. capricious. This epithet has been chosen on account of its popular derivation from the Latin *caper* (fem. *capra*), 'a goat.' The pun on 'goats' and 'Goths' would probably be very obvious to an Elizabethan audience because of the common sixteenth century pronunciation of *th*. In Thomas's *Historie of Italye*, 1561, 'Goths' is written 'gotes.' The allusion is, of course, to the banishment of Ovid to Tomi in the realm of the Getæ.

7. ill-inhabited : ill-lodged, having a bad habitation. See Abbott, § 294, on Verbs Passive. In J. C. Smith's edition of this play there is an excellent note on "Shakespeare's bold formations in *-ed*," and their twofold origin, the suffix being either adjectival or participial.

8. Ovid (*Metamorphoses*, VIII) tells how Jupiter and Mercury (Zeus and Hermes) were once overtaken by night in Phrygia, and were inhospitably excluded by all the people, till at last an old poor couple, named Philemon and Baucis, who lived in a thatched house, took them in and gave them the best entertainment the house would afford. Cf. *Much Ado About Nothing*, II, i, 99-100:

DON PEDRO. My visor is Philemon's roof; within the house is Jove.
HERO. Why, then, your visor should be thatch'd.

child, understanding, it strikes a man more dead than a
great reckoning in a little room. Truly, I would the gods
had made thee poetical.   13

AUDREY. I do not know what 'poetical' is : is it honest
in deed and word? is it a true thing?   15

TOUCHSTONE. No, truly; for the truest poetry is the
most feigning; and lovers are given to poetry; and what
they swear in poetry may be said as lovers they do feign.

AUDREY. Do you wish, then, that the gods had made me
poetical?   20

TOUCHSTONE. I do, truly; for thou swear'st to me thou
art honest: now, if thou wert a poet, I might have some
hope thou didst feign.

AUDREY. Would you not have me honest?   24

TOUCHSTONE. No, truly, unless thou wert hard-favour'd; for
honesty coupled to beauty is to have honey a sauce to sugar.

11-12. **a great reckoning in a little room.** Rabelais has a saying,
that "there is only one quarter of an hour in human life passed ill,
and that is between the calling for a reckoning and the paying it."
A heavy bill for narrow quarters is apt to dash the spirits of tavern
mirth. There is, as Singer remarks, "much humour in comparing
the blank countenance of a disappointed poet or wit, whose effu-
sions have not been comprehended, to that of the reveller who has
to pay largely for his carousing."

14-15. Of this speech of Audrey's Smetham wrote (*Letters*, 1891):
" I should like to have known that woman. She was a true Briton."

16. Cf. *A Midsummer Night's Dream*, V, 1, 14.

17-18. **what they swear in poetry may be said as lovers they do
feign.** In previous editions of Hudson's Shakespeare Mason's and
Collier's insertion of 'it' before 'may' was adopted. Johnson's conjecture is that the text should read, What they swear as lovers,
they may be said to feign as poets.

22. **honest**: virtuous. Cf. I, ii, 34, and 'dishonest' in V, iii, 4.

25. **hard-favour'd** . harsh-featured. Cf. I, ii, 33-35.

JAQUES. [*Aside*] A material fool !   27

AUDREY. Well, I am not fair; and therefore I pray the gods make me honest.   29

TOUCHSTONE. Truly, and to cast away honesty upon a foul slut were to put good meat into an unclean dish.

AUDREY. I am not a slut, though I thank the gods I am foul.   33

TOUCHSTONE. Well, prais'd be the gods for thy foulness ! sluttishness may come hereafter. But be it as it may be, I will marry thee, and to that end I have been with Sir Oliver Martext, the vicar of the next village, who hath promis'd to meet me in this place of the forest and to couple us.

JAQUES. [*Aside*] I would fain see this meeting.   39

AUDREY. Well, the gods give us joy !

TOUCHSTONE. Amen. A man may, if he were of a fearful heart, stagger in this attempt; for here we have no

27. material: full of matter. Cf. II, i, 68.

33. foul. Touchstone has just used this word in the ordinary sense of 'dirty,' but Audrey uses it as opposed to 'fair,' i.e. in the sense of 'plain,' 'homely.' She has good authority for doing so. Thus in Thomas's *Historie of Italye :* " If the maiden be faire, she is sone had, and little money geven with her; if she be foule, they avaunce hir with a better portion." So in *Sonnets,* CXXVII :

> For since each hand hath put on nature's power,
> Fairing the foul with art's false borrow'd face,
> Sweet beauty hath no name, no holy bower.

36. Sir. In common use as a clerical title in Shakespeare's time, and long before. Cf. Sir Hugh, the Welsh parson, in *The Merry Wives of Windsor*. Cf. Scott, *The Fair Maid of Perth*, Chapter XX : " . . . A priest and parson of St. John's, . . . like all the priests of the period (who were called from that circumstance the Pope's Knights), received the honourable title of *Dominus*, contracted into Dom, or Don, or translated into Sir, the title of reverence due to the secular chivalry."

temple but the wood, no assembly but horn-beasts. But
what though? Courage! As horns are odious, they are
necessary. It is said, 'Many a man knows no end of his
goods': right! many a man has good horns, and knows
no end of them. Well, that is the dowry of his wife; 't is
none of his own getting. Horns? — even so: — poor men
alone? No, no; the noblest deer hath them as huge as
the rascal. Is the single man therefore bless'd? No: as a
wall'd town is more worthier than a village, so is the forehead of a married man more honourable than the bare brow
of a bachelor; and by how much defence is better than no
skill, by so much is a horn more precious than to want.
Here comes Sir Oliver. —   55

Enter SIR OLIVER MARTEXT

Sir Oliver Martext, you are well met: will you dispatch us
here under this tree, or shall we go with you to your
chapel?   58

---

43. horn-beasts   F3F4 | horne-
beasts F1F2 | horn'd beasts Walker
conj.

48-49. Horns? — even so: — poor
men alone? Theobald Camb | hornes,
even so poore men alone: Ff.

43. **horn-beasts**. Walker's suggestion that this should be 'horn'd
beasts,' a final _d_ and final _e_ having been confounded, was adopted
in previous editions of Hudson's Shakespeare. But the Folio reading gives an expression often heard to-day in the North of England.

48-49. In previous editions of Hudson's Shakespeare the reading,
'Horns given to poor men alone?' was adopted; but in the present
text the Theobald emendation is followed. It makes the least
change upon the Folio reading and is in perfect keeping with the
spirit of Touchstone's speech.

50. **rascal**: deer out of condition. See Skeat and Century.

54. In _The Merchant of Venice_, V, i, 47, there is a similar quibble
upon a postman's 'horn' and the 'horn of plenty.'

SIR OLIVER. Is there none here to give the woman?

TOUCHSTONE. I will not take her on gift of any man. 60

SIR OLIVER. Truly, she must be given, or the marriage is not lawful.

JAQUES. [*Coming forward*] Proceed, proceed: I 'll give her.   64

TOUCHSTONE. Good even, good Master What-ye-call 't : how do you, sir? You are very well met : God 'ild you for your last company : I am very glad to see you : — even a toy in hand here, sir ; — nay, pray be cover'd.   68

JAQUES. Will you be married, motley?

TOUCHSTONE. As the ox hath his bow, sir, the horse his curb, and the falcon her bells, so man hath his desires ; and as pigeons bill, so wedlock would be nibbling.   72

JAQUES. And will you, being a man of your breeding, be married under a bush, like a beggar? Get you to church, and have a good priest that can tell you what marriage is : this fellow will but join you together as they join wainscot ; then one of you will prove a shrunk panel, and like green timber warp, warp.   78

TOUCHSTONE. [*Aside*] I am not in the mind but I were better to be married of him than of another : for he is not

---

66. God 'ild Theobald | goddild
F₁ | godild F₂F₃F₄.

71. her bells F₁F₂ | his bells F₃F₄.
79. [*Aside*] Capell.

66. **God 'ild** : God yield, God reward. So again in V, iv, 53.

68. **be cover'd.** Jaques is supposed to be standing with his hat off, out of deference to the present company. Cf. V, i, 17.

70. **bow** : bow-shaped part of a yoke. It fitted the neck.

71. The falcon is strictly the female hawk, — the " gay gos-hawk, a bird o' high degree," — as distinguished from the male, a smaller bird, known in falconry as a 'tercel,' 'tiercel,' or 'tiercelet.'

79–80. **but I were better.** That it were not better for me.

like to marry me well; and not being well married, it will
be a good excuse for me hereafter to leave my wife.   82

JAQUES. Go thou with me, and let me counsel thee.

TOUCHSTONE. Come, sweet Audrey:

Farewell, good Master Oliver; not, —   85

> O sweet Oliver,
> O brave Oliver,
> Leave me not behind thee;

but, —

> Wind away,   90
> Be gone, I say,
> I will not to wedding with thee.

[*Exeunt* JAQUES, TOUCHSTONE, *and* AUDREY]

SIR OLIVER. 'T is no matter: ne'er a fantastical knave
of them all shall flout me out of my calling.   [*Exit*]

SCENE IV. *The forest*

Enter ROSALIND *and* CELIA

ROSALIND. Never talk to me; I will weep.

CELIA. Do, I prithee; but yet have the grace to consider that tears do not become a man.   3

---

83. Printed as two lines in Ff.   90-92. Printed as prose in Ff.
86-88. Printed as prose in Ff.   SCENE IV | Scene X Pope.

86. Touchstone's snatches of song are probably from an Elizabethan ballad, "O swete Olyver, Leave me not behind the," entered
in *The Stationers' Registers* in 1584 and 1586. This ballad seems to
have been in two parts, for in the *Registers* there is reference to
"the answeare of O swete Olyver." Touchstone says, I will sing, not
that part of the ballad which says, "Leave me not behind thee";
but that which says, "Be gone, I say," probably part of the answer.
90. wind: turn and go. Connected etymologically with 'wend.'

ROSALIND. But have I not cause to weep?

CELIA. As good cause as one would desire ; therefore weep.   6

ROSALIND. His very hair is of the dissembling colour.

CELIA. Something browner than Judas's : marry, his kisses are Judas's own children.

ROSALIND. I' faith, his hair is of a good colour.   10

CELIA. An excellent colour : your chestnut was ever the only colour.

ROSALIND. And his kissing is as full of sanctity as the touch of holy bread.   14

CELIA. He hath bought a pair of cast lips of Diana : a nun of winter's sisterhood kisses not more religiously ; the very ice of chastity is in them.   17

ROSALIND. But why did he swear he would come this morning, and comes not?

CELIA. Nay, certainly, there is no truth in him.

ROSALIND. Do you think so?   21

CELIA. Yes ; I think he is not a pick-purse nor a horse-stealer ; but for his verity in love, I do think him as concave as a covered goblet or a worm-eaten nut.

5-17. Printed as twelve lines of verse in Ff.

15. cast F1 | chast F2F3F4 | chaste Rowe Pope.

8. In old paintings and tapestry Judas was represented with red hair and beard. The red wig of Judas was a famous stage property in the old miracle plays. So arose the stage tradition.

15. cast. Rowe's reading 'chaste' was adopted in previous editions of Hudson's Shakespeare. But 'cast' in the sense of 'discarded' is in keeping with the teasing spirit Celia shows in this scene. There is probably, too, a quibble upon 'cast' and 'chaste' — the common epithet applied to Diana.

17. ice of chastity. Cf. *Coriolanus*, V, iii, 64–67.

ROSALIND. Not true in love?   25

CELIA. Yes, when he is in; but I think he is not in.

ROSALIND. You have heard him swear downright he was.

CELIA. 'Was' is not 'is': besides, the oath of a lover is
no stronger than the word of a tapster; they are both the
confirmer of false reckonings. He attends here in the forest
on the Duke your father.   31

ROSALIND. I met the Duke yesterday, and had much
question with him: he ask'd me of what parentage I was;
I told him, of as good as he; so he laugh'd and let me go.
But what talk we of fathers, when there is such a man as
Orlando?   36

CELIA. O, that's a brave man! he writes brave verses,
speaks brave words, swears brave oaths and breaks them
bravely, quite traverse, athwart the heart of his lover; as a
puisny tilter, that spurs his horse but on one side, breaks
his staff like a noble goose: but all's brave that youth
mounts and folly guides.— Who comes here?   42

28. a lover F₂F₃F₄ | lover F₁.   30. confirmer Ff | confirmers Pope.

28. So the ancient proverb, "At lovers' perjuries Jove laughs."

33. question : conversation. Often so in Shakespeare.

39. An allusion to tilting, where it was held disgraceful for a knight
to break his lance across the body of his adversary, instead of by a
push of the point. Cf. *Much Ado About Nothing*, V, i, 139.— traverse :
across.— lover : mistress. So in *Cymbeline*, V, v, 172.

40. puisny : inferior, unskillful. This is the Old French word *puisné*
(modern French *puiné*), 'younger,' from Lat. *post-natum*. The word
survives in two forms in modern English : 'puisne' in the expression 'puisne judge,' and 'puny' in the sense of 'small,' 'petty.'

41. noble. Hanmer substituted 'nose-quill'd,' and Singer 'not-
able,' but 'noble' is here used ironically. Caldecott suggests that
by the phrase 'noble goose' is meant a 'magnanimous simpleton of
an adventurer.'

Enter CORIN

CORIN. Mistress and master, you have oft inquir'd
After the shepherd that complain'd of love,
Who you saw sitting by me on the turf,   45
Praising the proud disdainful shepherdess
That was his mistress.
CELIA.   Well, and what of him?
CORIN. If you will see a pageant truly play'd,
Between the pale complexion of true love
And the red glow of scorn and proud disdain,   50
Go hence a little and I shall conduct you,
If you will mark it.
ROSALIND.   O, come, let us remove:
The sight of lovers feedeth those in love. —
Bring us to this sight, and you shall say   54
I 'll prove a busy actor in their play.   [*Exeunt*]

SCENE V. *Another part of the forest*

Enter SILVIUS *and* PHEBE

SILVIUS. Sweet Phebe, do not scorn me; do not, Phebe:
Say that you love me not, but say not so
In bitterness. The common executioner,
Whose heart the accustom'd sight of death makes hard,
Falls not the axe upon the humbled neck   5

---

45. **Who** F1 | Whom F2F3F4. to this Capell | Bring us unto this
54. **Bring us to this** Ff | Bring us Malone | Bring us to see this Dyce.
but to this Pope | Come, bring us SCENE V | Scene XI Pope.

5. **Falls not**: lets not fall. Shakespeare more than once uses
'fall' transitively. Cf. *Lucrece*, 1551; *The Tempest*, V, i, 64.

But first begs pardon : will you sterner be
Than he that dies and lives by bloody drops?

Enter ROSALIND, CELIA, *and* CORIN, *behind*

PHEBE. I would not be thy executioner :
I fly thee, for I would not injure thee.
Thou tell'st me there is murder in mine eye :   10
'T is pretty, sure, and very probable,
That eyes, that are the frail'st and softest things,
Who shut their coward gates on atomies,
Should be call'd tyrants, butchers, murderers !
Now I do frown on thee with all my heart ;   15
And if mine eyes can wound, now let them kill thee :
Now counterfeit to swoon ; why, now fall down ;
Or if thou canst not, O, for shame, for shame,

7. **dies and lives** Ff | deals and
lives Theobald | lives and thrives
Hanmer | lives and dies Keightley.

11. **pretty, sure,** Theobald |
pretty sure Ff.

17. **swoon** Rowe | swound Ff.

6. It was customary for the executioner to kneel down and ask
pardon of the victim before striking him.

7. This is a phrase of frequent occurrence in old writers, and
seems to have been an idiomatic *hysteron proteron* for 'live and die.'
The explanation given by Dr. Sebastian Evans to Dr. C. M. Ingleby
is noteworthy : " It means, of course, to 'make the thing a matter of
life and death.' The profession or calling of a man is that by which
he dies and lives ; that is, by which he lives, and failing which he dies."

11. **pretty, sure.** Dr. Furness notes the comic turn given to the
phrase in the text of the First Folio by the omission of the comma
after 'pretty.'

17. 'Swoon' occurs three times in this play, and each time the
First Folio spells it differently. — 'swound' here, 'swoon' in IV, iii,
158, and 'sound' in V, ii, 25 : evidence, as Dr. Furness says, that the
pronunciation of the word "was in a transition state when the Folio
was printing."

Lie not, to say mine eyes are murderers !
Now show the wound mine eye hath made in thee :   20
Scratch thee but with a pin, and there remains
Some scar of it ; lean but upon a rush,
The cicatrice and capable impressure
Thy palm some moment keeps : but now mine eyes,
Which I have darted at thee, hurt thee not ;   25
Nor, I am sure, there is no force in eyes
That can do hurt.

    SILVIUS.   O dear Phebe,
If ever, — as that ever may be near, —
You meet in some fresh cheek the power of fancy,
Then shall you know the wounds invisible   30
That love's keen arrows make.

    PHEBE.   ·   But till that time
Come not thou near me ; and when that time comes,
Afflict me with thy mocks, pity me not ;
As till that time I shall not pity thee.

    ROSALIND. [*Advancing*] And why, I pray you? Who
           might be your mother,   35
That you insult, exult, and all at once,
Over the wretched? What though you have no beauty, —

---

22. **but** omitted in F1.

37. **have no** | hau no F1 | have   mo Malone | have more Steevens | have some Hanmer.

23. **capable impressure** : sensible impression. Singer and Collier's second folio change 'capable' to 'palpable.' But elsewhere, as in *Hamlet*, III, iv, 127, Shakespeare uses 'capable' as passive. Cf. 'incapable' for 'insensible' or 'unconscious,' in *Hamlet*, IV, vii, 178–179 :

> she chanted snatches of old tunes ;
> As one incapable of her own distress.

29. **fancy** : love. So 'fancy-monger,' III, ii, 341, and 'fancy-free,' *A Midsummer Night's Dream*, II, i, 164.

As, by my faith, I see no more in you
Than without candle may go dark to bed, —
Must you be therefore proud and pitiless?   40
Why, what means this? Why do you look on me?
I see no more in you than in the ordinary
Of nature's sale-work. 'Od's my little life,
I think she means to tangle my eyes too !
No, faith, proud mistress, hope not after it: 45
'T is not your inky brows, your black silk hair,
Your bugle eyeballs, nor your cheek of cream,
That can entame my spirits to your worship.
You foolish shepherd, wherefore do you follow her,
Like foggy south, puffing with wind and rain?   50
You are a thousand times a properer man
Than she a woman : 't is such fools as you
That makes the world full of ill-favour'd children :
'T is not her glass, but you, that flatters her ;
And out of you she sees herself more proper   55

40. Rosalind knows that to tell Phebe she ought not to be proud
because she has beauty would but make her the prouder; she therefore tells her she ought not to be proud because she lacks it. Often
the best way to take down people's pride is to assume that they cannot be so big fools as to think they have anything to be proud of.

43. nature's sale-work. The expression has reference, apparently,
to work made for the general market, and not to particular order or
for any special purpose or purchaser. —'Od's my little life. A petty
oath, in which ''Od's' is a diminutive, or disguise, of 'God's.' Cf.
''Od's my will,' IV, iii, 17 ; ''Od's heartlings,' *The Merry Wives of
Windsor*, III, iv, 59 ; ''Od's lifelings,' *Twelfth Night*, V, i, 187 ;
''Od's pittikins,' *Cymbeline*, IV, ii, 293.

47. bugle eyeballs : eyes black as bugles. 'Bugles' were beads of
elongated glass, often black. Cf. 'bugle bracelet,' in the song of
Autolycus, *The Winter's Tale*, IV, iv, 224.

51. properer : handsomer. So in ll. 55, 114, and in I, ii, 106.

Than any of her lineaments can show her.
But, mistress, know yourself : down on your knees,
And thank heaven, fasting, for a good man's love :
For I must tell you friendly in your ear,
Sell when you can : you are not for all markets :   60
Cry the man mercy ; love him ; take his offer :
Foul is most foul, being foul to be a scoffer. —
So, take her to thee, shepherd ; fare you well.

PHEBE. Sweet youth, I pray you, chide a year together :
I had rather hear you chide than this man woo.   65

ROSALIND. He 's fallen in love with your foulness and
she 'll fall in love with my anger. If it be so, as fast as she
answers thee with frowning looks, I 'll sauce her with bitter
words. — Why look you so upon me?

PHEBE. For no ill will I bear you.   70

ROSALIND. I pray you, do not fall in love with me,
For I am falser than vows made in wine :
Besides, I like you not. If you will know my house,
'T is at the tuft of olives here hard by. —
Will you go, sister? — Shepherd, ply her hard. —   75
Come, sister. — Shepherdess, look on him better,
And be not proud : though all the world could see,
None could be so abus'd in sight as he. —
Come, to our flock.   [*Exeunt* ROSALIND, CELIA, *and* CORIN]

66-69. Printed as verse in Ff.   77. see Ff | see ye Hanmer.
66. your Ff | her Hanmer.   79. Come, to F1F2 | Come to F3F4.

61. **Cry the man mercy** : beg the man's pardon.
62. **to be.** If this is an instance of the infinitive used gerundively (Abbott, § 356), the meaning is, The ugly are most ugly when
they add further ugliness by being scoffers, or scornful.
77-78. If all men could see you, none but he could be so deceived
as to think you beautiful.

PHEBE. Dead shepherd, now I find thy saw of might, —
' Who ever lov'd that lov'd not at first sight? '   81
   SILVIUS. Sweet Phebe, —
   PHEBE.   Ha, what say'st thou, Silvius?
   SILVIUS. Sweet Phebe, pity me.
   PHEBE. Why, I am sorry for thee, gentle Silvius.
   SILVIUS. Wherever sorrow is, relief would be :   85
If you do sorrow at my grief in love,
By giving love your sorrow and my grief
Were both extermin'd.
   PHEBE. Thou hast my love : is not that neighbourly?
   SILVIUS. I would have you.
   PHEBE.   Why, that were covetousness.
Silvius, the time was that I hated thee,   91
And yet it is not that I bear thee love ;
But since that thou canst talk of love so well,
Thy company, which erst was irksome to me,
I will endure ; and I 'll employ thee too :   95
But do not look for further recompense
Than thine own gladness that thou art employ'd.
   SILVIUS. So holy and so perfect is my love,
And I in such a poverty of grace,
That I shall think it a most plenteous crop   100

---

80. **Dead** F1 | Deed F2F3F4 | 99. **And I in** F1 | And in F2 | And
'Deed Hanmer | Dear Gould conj.   F3F4.

80. **Dead shepherd.** The obvious reference is to Christopher
Marlowe, the 'saw of might' in the succeeding line being from his
Hero and Leander, first printed in 1598. While the pastoral convention (see Introduction, page x) so influenced Elizabethan literature
that the word 'shepherd' became a synonym for 'poet,' the expression 'dead shepherd' has about it a ring of personal affection.

88. **extermin'd:** exterminated. Cf. Fr. *exterminer*.

To glean the broken ears after the man
That the main harvest reaps : loose now and then
A scatter'd smile, and that I'll live upon.

   PHEBE. Know'st thou the youth that spoke to me ere-
       while?

   SILVIUS. Not very well, but I have met him oft ;   105
And he hath bought the cottage and the bounds
That the old carlot once was master of.

   PHEBE. Think not I love him, though I ask for him ;
'T is but a peevish boy ; yet he talks well ;
But what care I for words? yet words do well   110
When he that speaks them pleases those that hear.
It is a pretty youth — not very pretty ;
But, sure, he's proud ; and yet his pride becomes him :
He'll make a proper man : the best thing in him
Is his complexion ; and faster than his tongue   115
Did make offence, his eye did heal·it up.
He is not very tall ; yet for his years he's tall :
His leg is but so so ; and yet 't is well :
There was a pretty redness in his lip,
A little riper and more lusty red   120
Than that mix'd in his cheek ; 't was just the difference
Betwixt the constant red and mingled damask.

102. loose F₁F₂F₃ | lose F₄ Rowe.   117. very omitted by Hanmer
104. erewhile F₄ | yerewhile F₁F₂F₃.   Capell Steevens.

107. carlot: peasant. Probably a word of Shakespearian coinage
—a diminutive of 'carl' or 'churl.' Cf. II, iv, 75.
122. mingled damask. Cf. *Sonnets*, CXXX, 5 ; *The Passionate Pil-
grim*, 89 ; *Love's Labour's Lost*, V, ii, 296 ; *Twelfth Night*, II, iv, 115.
Shakespeare, like Tennyson, uses the word 'damask' in two senses,
one having reference to the rose, and the other to the rich varie-
gated fabric of that name.

There be some women, Silvius, had they mark'd him
In parcels as I did, would have gone near
To fall in love with him : but, for my part,   125
I love him not, nor hate him not; and yet
I have more cause to hate him than to love him :
For what had he to do to chide at me?
He said mine eyes were black, and my hair black;
And, now I am remember'd, scorn'd at me :   130
I marvel why I answer'd not again :
But that 's all one ; omittance is no quittance.
I 'll write to him a very taunting letter,
And thou shalt bear it; wilt thou, Silvius?   134
    SILVIUS. Phebe, with all my heart.

    PHEBE.   I 'll write it straight ;
The matter 's in my head and in my heart :
I will be bitter with him and passing short.
Go with me, Silvius.   [*Exeunt*]

---

127. **I have** F2F3F4 | Have F1.   133. **taunting** F4 | tanting F1F2F3.

124. **in parcels** : in detail. 'Parcel' etymologically means 'portion.'
128. What business had he to chide me as he did?
130. **am remember'd** : recollect. Cf. *Measure for Measure*, II, i, 110.
132. **omittance is no quittance.** This is evidently a proverb. 'Omittance,' as a legal term, meant in the sixteenth century, formal discharge from a debt or obligation. It then came to mean 'repayment,' 'recompense,' as in *2 Henry IV*, I, i, 108. Cf. the proverbial expression, 'cry quittance,' meaning 'get even ':

      Cry quittance, madam, then, and love not him.
                 Marlowe, *Edward II*, I, iv.

135. **straight** : straightway, immediately. So in *Hamlet*, V, i, 4.
137. **passing short** : extremely curt. 'Passing' is still used in poetry for 'surpassingly,' 'exceedingly':

      For she was passing weary of his love.
              Matthew Arnold, *Tristram and Iseult*.

ACT IV

Scene I. *The forest*

Enter Rosalind, Celia, *and* Jaques

Jaques. I prithee, pretty youth, let me be better acquainted with thee.

Rosalind. They say you are a melancholy fellow.

Jaques. I am so; I do love it better than laughing.   4

Rosalind. Those that are in extremity of either are abominable fellows, and betray themselves to every modern censure worse than drunkards.

Jaques. Why, 't is good to be sad and say nothing.

Rosalind. Why, then 't is good to be a post.   9

Jaques. I have neither the scholar's melancholy, which is emulation; nor the musician's, which is fantastical; nor the courtier's, which is proud; nor the soldier's, which is ambitious; nor the lawyer's, which is politic; nor the lady's, which is nice; nor the lover's, which is all these; but it is a melancholy of mine own, compounded of many simples, extracted from many objects, and, indeed, the sundry

---

The forest Rowe | Ff omit.
1. **me be better** F₂F₃F₄ | me better F₁.

6. **abominable** F₄ | abhominable F₁.

13. **politic** | political Rowe.

5. **in extremity of**: extremely given to. Cf. IV, iii, 23.
6. **modern**: ordinary. Cf. II, vii, 155.
7. **censure**: judgment. But in l. 171 it means 'blame.'
14. **nice**: fastidious. From Lat. *nescius* through Old Fr. *nice*.
15. **simples**: element ingredients. Usually herbs.

contemplation of my travels, in which my often rumination wraps me in a most humorous sadness.   18

ROSALIND. A traveller! By my faith, you have great reason to be sad : I fear you have sold your own lands to see other men's ; then, to have seen much, and to have nothing, is to have rich eyes and poor hands.

JAQUES. Yes, I have gain'd my experience.   23

ROSALIND. And your experience makes you sad : I had rather have a fool to make me merry than experience to make me sad ; and to travel for it too !

Enter ORLANDO

ORLANDO. Good day and happiness, dear Rosalind !   27

JAQUES. Nay, then, God be wi' you, and you talk in blank verse !   [*Exit*]

17. **contemplation** F₁ | contemplations F₃F₄.—**in which my** F₂F₃F₄ | in which by F₁.

27. *Enter* ORLANDO in Ff after l. 23.

28. **be wi' you** | buy you Ff.

17–18. The text follows the later Folios, and the probable construction is — " my often rumination in which (travels) wraps me . . ." In an endeavor to emend the text, Singer and Dyce threw out the 'in' altogether, and retained 'by,' making 'which' the subject of 'wraps.' In previous editions of Hudson's Shakespeare the Jervis-Seymour reading, 'on which my,' was adopted.

18. **humorous**: whimsical. See note, p. 25, l. 246.

28. **be wi' you.** See note, p. 79, l. 244. — **and** : if. So in ll. 36, 46, 64. This is the reading of the Folios. Pope read 'an,' but the change is unnecessary. See Murray, 'and,' and Abbott, § 101.

28–29. **blank verse.** This expression, used by Nash in the Preface to Greene's *Menaphon*, 1589, Shakespeare employs three times.

29. This *Exit* is not marked in the First Folio, but appears in the other Folios. In previous editions of Hudson's Shakespeare '*Exit* JAQUES' is inserted after 'gondola,' l. 34. This suggestion was first made by Dyce and is defended by Dr. Furness.

ROSALIND. Farewell, Monsieur Traveller : look you lisp and wear strange suits ; disable all the benefits of your own country ; be out of love with your nativity and almost chide God for making you that countenance you are ; or I will scarce think you have swam in a gondola. — Why, how now, Orlando ! where have you been all this while ? You a lover ! And you serve me such another trick, never come in my sight more.   37

ORLANDO. My fair Rosalind, I come within an hour of my promise.   39

ROSALIND. Break an hour's promise in love ! He that will divide a minute into a thousand parts, and break but a part of the thousandth part of a minute in the affairs of love, it may be said of him that Cupid hath clapp'd him o' the shoulder, but I 'll warrant him heart-whole.   44

ORLANDO. Pardon me, dear Rosalind.

ROSALIND. Nay, and you be so tardy, come no more in my sight : I had as lief be woo'd of a snail.

30. Scene II Pope.
34. gondola Pope | Gundello Ff.
42. thousandth Rowe | thousand Ff.

44. heart-whole Rowe | heart whole F₄ | heart hole F₁F₂F₃.

31. strange suits. Similar satire of the affectation of foreign dress is in *Much Ado About Nothing*, III, ii, 35, and *The Merchant of Venice*, I, ii, 79. — disable : disparage. Cf. V, iv, 72.

33. Cf. *Sonnets*, XXIX, 5–6 : " Wishing me . . . Featur'd like him."

34. In Shakespeare's time Venice, on account of its gayety, was the common resort of travelers, as much as Paris is now. And of course all who went to Venice sailed or ' swam in a gondola.' Cf. *The Merchant of Venice*, II, viii, 8.

43–44. clapp'd him o' the shoulder. In *Troilus and Cressida*, III, iii, 139 ; *Love's Labour 's Lost*, V, ii, 107 ; and *Much Ado About Nothing*, I, i, 261, this expression is used to signify friendly encouragement. This is probably the meaning here. In *Cymbeline*, V, iii, 78, a similar expression, ' touch my shoulder,' means ' arrest.'

ORLANDO. Of a snail?   48

ROSALIND. Ay, of a snail; for, though he comes slowly, he carries his house on his head, — a better jointure, I think, than you make a woman: besides, he brings his destiny with him.   52

ORLANDO. What's that?

ROSALIND. Why, horns; which such as you are fain to be beholding to your wives for: but he comes arm'd in his fortune and prevents the slander of his wife.   56

ORLANDO. Virtue is no horn-maker; and my Rosalind is virtuous.

ROSALIND. And I am your Rosalind.   59

CELIA. It pleases him to call you so; but he hath a Rosalind of a better leer than you.   61

ROSALIND. Come, woo me, woo me; for now I am in a holiday humour, and like enough to consent. What would you say to me now, and I were your very very Rosalind?

ORLANDO. I would kiss before I spoke.   65

ROSALIND. Nay, you were better speak first; and when you were gravell'd for lack of matter, you might take

55. **beholding**: beholden. A common sixteenth century corruption.

56. **prevents**: anticipates. Often so in Elizabethan literature. — **the slander of his wife**: the slander caused by his wife.

61. **leer**: aspect, mien. This word (Middle English *lere* or *lire*, Anglo-Saxon *hleór*, 'cheek') Shakespeare uses in two senses: (1) 'mien,' 'look,' 'complexion,' as here and in *Titus Andronicus*, IV, ii, 119; (2) 'a sly or amorous look,' as in *The Merry Wives of Windsor*, I, iii, 50. It is possible that Celia uses the word here in the double sense.

67. **gravell'd**: stuck, stranded. It has been suggested that this use of 'gravel' sprang from horses being lamed, as they sometimes are, by getting gravel-stones into their hoofs. More likely, however, is the suggestion in Cotgrave: "*Assablé:* gravelled; filled with sand; also stuck in, or run on, the sand."

occasion to kiss. Very good orators, when they are out, they
will spit; and for lovers, lacking — God warn us! — matter,
the cleanliest shift is to kiss.   70

ORLANDO. How if the kiss be denied?

ROSALIND. Then she puts you to entreaty and there
begins new matter.

ORLANDO. Who could be out, being before his belov'd
mistress?   75

ROSALIND. Marry, that should you, if I were your mistress; or I should think my honesty ranker than my wit.

ORLANDO. What, of my suit?

ROSALIND. Not out of your apparel, and yet out of your
suit. Am not I your Rosalind?   80

ORLANDO. I take some joy to say you are, because I
would be talking of her.

ROSALIND. Well, in her person, I say, I will not have you.

ORLANDO. Then in mine own person, I die.   84

ROSALIND. No, faith, die by attorney. The poor world
is almost six thousand years old, and in all this time there
was not any man died in his own person, videlicet, in a
love-cause. Troilus had his brains dash'd out with a Grecian
club; yet he did what he could to die before; and he is
one of the patterns of love. Leander, he would have liv'd
many a fair year, though Hero had turn'd nun, if it had not
been for a hot midsummer night; for, good youth, he went
but forth to wash him in the Hellespont, and, being taken

---

84. die F_1 | doe F_2F_3.   93. him F_1 | omitted in $F_2F_3F_4$.

85. by attorney: by deputy or substitute. 'Attorney' (Old Fr. *a*,
'to,' Lat. *ad*, and *torner*, 'to turn') is defined by Skeat as "an agent
who acts in the 'turn' of another."

88–94. Rosalind invents the Grecian club and Leander's cramp.

with the cramp, was drown'd : and the foolish chroniclers
of that age found it was — Hero of Sestos. But these are
all lies : men have died from time to time and worms
have eaten them, but not for love. 97

ORLANDO. I would not have my right Rosalind of this
mind ; for, I protest, her frown might kill me. 99

ROSALIND. By this hand, it will not kill a fly. But come,
now I will be your Rosalind in a more coming-on disposition ; and ask me what you will, I will grant it. 102

ORLANDO. Then love me, Rosalind.

ROSALIND. Yes, faith, will I, Fridays and Saturdays and all.

ORLANDO. And wilt thou have me? 105

ROSALIND. Ay, and twenty such.

ORLANDO. What say'st thou?

ROSALIND. Are you not good?

ORLANDO. I hope so. 109

ROSALIND. Why, then, can one desire too much of a good
thing? — Come, sister, you shall be the priest and marry us.
— Give me your hand, Orlando. — What do you say, sister?

ORLANDO. Pray thee, marry us.

CELIA. I cannot say the words. 114

ROSALIND. You must begin, ' Will you, Orlando, —'

CELIA. Go to. — Will you, Orlando, have to wife this
Rosalind? 117

94. **chroniclers** F₂F₈F₄ | chronoclers F₁ | coroners Hanmer.

95. **found** : brought in a verdict. The verdict was, 'drowned himself for love of Hero.' The report of the old chroniclers or histo-
rians is implicitly compared to the finding of a coroner's inquest. Cf.
Hamlet, V, i, 5. For a discussion of Hanmer's famous substitution
of 'coroners' for 'chroniclers,' see Furness.

101. **more coming-on disposition** : a disposition more facile, ready,
and encouraging. 'Coming-on' is probably a Shakespeare coinage.

ORLANDO. I will.

ROSALIND. Ay, but when?

ORLANDO. Why, now; as fast as she can marry us.   120

ROSALIND. Then you must say, 'I take thee, Rosalind, for wife.'

ORLANDO. I take thee, Rosalind, for wife.   123

ROSALIND. I might ask you for your commission; but, I do take thee, Orlando, for my husband: there's a girl goes before the priest; and, certainly, a woman's thought runs before her actions.   127

ORLANDO. So do all thoughts; they are wing'd.

ROSALIND. Now tell me how long you would have her after you have possess'd her.

ORLANDO. For ever and a day.   131

ROSALIND. Say 'a day,' without the 'ever.' No, no, Orlando; men are April when they woo, December when they wed: maids are May when they are maids, but the sky changes when they are wives. I will be more jealous of thee than a Barbary cock-pigeon over his hen, more clamorous than a parrot against rain, more new-fangl'd than an ape, more giddy in my desires than a monkey: I will weep for nothing, like Diana in the fountain; and I will do that

124. **commission**: warrant. Authority to perform the marriage ceremony; or, warrant for 'taking' me to wife.

126. **goes before the priest**: goes faster than the priest. Rosalind gets ahead of the priest in the service.

136. **Barbary.** "'Barbary' of itself implies Oriental watchfulness and jealousy." — Furness.

137. **new-fangl'd.** For the interesting history of this word, see Skeat.

139. **Diana in the fountain.** Figures of Diana were anciently a frequent ornament of fountains. So in *The City Match:* "Now could I

when you are dispos'd to be merry: I will laugh like a hyen, and that when thou art inclin'd to sleep. 141

ORLANDO. But will my Rosalind do so?

ROSALIND. By my life, she will do as I do.

ORLANDO. O, but she is wise. 144

ROSALIND. Or else she could not have the wit to do this: the wiser, the waywarder: make the doors upon a woman's wit and it will out at the casement; shut that, and 't will out at the key-hole; stop that, 't will fly with the smoke out at the chimney. 149

ORLANDO. A man that had a wife with such a wit, he might say, 'Wit, whither wilt?'

ROSALIND. You shall never take her without her answer, unless you take her without her tongue. O, that woman that cannot make her fault her husband's occasion, let her never nurse her child herself, for she will breed it like a fool! 155

ORLANDO. For these two hours, Rosalind, I will leave thee.

ROSALIND. Alas, dear love, I cannot lack thee two hours!

ORLANDO. I must attend the Duke at dinner: by two o'clock I will be with thee again. 159

ROSALIND. Ay, go your ways, go your ways: I knew what

cry like any image in a fountain which runs lamentations." According to Stowe, such an image of Diana with "water conveyed from the Thames prilling from her naked breast" was set up at the Cross in Cheapside in 1596.

140. hyen: hyena. The bark of the hyena, "a feigning of man's voice," was thought to resemble a loud laugh.

146. make: shut close. So in *The Comedy of Errors*, III, i, 93.

151. 'Wit, whither wilt?' An old proverbial saying, probably meaning, Whither will your wit lead you? Cf. I, ii, 50.

154. husband's occasion. Hanmer changed 'occasion' to 'accusation.' The text as it stands probably means, "that cannot represent or make out that her husband was the occasion of her fault."

you would prove ; my friends told me as much, and I thought
no less. That flattering tongue of yours won me : 't is but one
cast away, and so,—come, death ! Two o'clock is your hour?

ORLANDO. Ay, sweet Rosalind.   164

ROSALIND. By my troth, and in good earnest, and so God
mend me, and by all pretty oaths that are not dangerous,
if you break one jot of your promise, or come one minute
behind your hour, I will think you the most pathetical break-
promise, and the most hollow lover, and the most unworthy
of her you call Rosalind, that may be chosen out of the
gross band of the unfaithful : therefore beware my censure
and keep your promise.   172

ORLANDO. With no less religion than if thou wert indeed
my Rosalind : so adieu.   174

ROSALIND. Well, Time is the old justice that examines all
such offenders, and let Time try : adieu. [*Exit* ORLANDO]

CELIA. You have simply misus'd our sex in your love-
prate : we must have your doublet and hose pluck'd over
your head, and show the world what the bird hath done to
her own nest.   180

177. Scene III Pope.

168. **pathetical.** This word, used by Lodge in describing Phebe's
indifference to Montanus, meant sometimes 'full of passion' and
'sentimental,' as well as 'affection-moving.' Rosalind is using it play-
fully, with mock seriousness. Warburton substituted 'atheistical'!

175. **Time is the old justice.** Cf. *Troilus and Cressida*, IV, v, 224 :

the end crowns all,
And that old common arbitrator, Time,
Will one day end it.

177. **misus'd** : abused. So in *Much Ado About Nothing*, II, i, 246.
178. "I pray, quoth Aliena, if your robes were off, what mettal
are you made of that you are so satyrical against women ? is it not
a foule bird that defiles its own nest ? " — Lodge's *Rosalynde.*

ROSALIND. O coz, coz, coz, my pretty little coz, that thou didst know how many fathom deep I am in love ! But it cannot be sounded : my affection hath an unknown bottom, like the bay of Portugal.   184

CELIA. Or rather, bottomless; that as fast as you pour affection in, it runs out.   186

ROSALIND. No, that same wicked bastard of Venus that was begot of thought, conceiv'd of spleen, and born of madness, that blind rascally boy that abuses every one's eyes because his own are out, let him be judge how deep I am in love. I 'll tell thee, Aliena, I cannot be out of the sight of Orlando : I 'll go find a shadow and sigh till he come.

CELIA. And I 'll sleep.   [*Exeunt*]

SCENE II. *The forest*

Enter JAQUES, Lords, *and* Foresters

JAQUES. Which is he that kill'd the deer?

A LORD. Sir, it was I.

JAQUES. Let 's present him to the Duke, like a Roman

SCENE II | Scene IV Pope.   2. A LORD | Lord Ff Malone.

192. **shadow** : a shady place. Cf. *Macbeth*, IV, iii, 1 ; *The Tempest*, IV, i, 67 ; *Venus and Adonis*, 191.

SCENE II. " This noisy scene was introduced to fill up an interval which is to represent two hours." — Johnson. Flower, in his *Memorial Theatre Edition*, has the following interesting note in connection with this scene : " On the occasion of the first representation of *As You Like It* in the Memorial Theatre, Stratford, April 30, 1879, a fallow deer was carried on the stage by foresters, which had been that morning shot by H. S. Lucy, Esq., of Charlecote Park, of the herd descended from that upon which Shakespeare is credited with having made a raid in his youth. The deer is now stuffed and carried on whenever the play is acted in Stratford."

conqueror; and it would do well to set the deer's horns
upon his head, for a branch of victory. — Have you no
song, forester, for this purpose?   6

FORESTER. Yes, sir.

JAQUES. Sing it: 'tis no matter how it be in tune, so it
make noise enough.

SONG

FORESTER. What shall he have that kill'd the deer?   10
         His leather skin, and horns to wear.
         Then sing him home:
              [*The rest shall bear this burthen*]
         Take thou no scorn to wear the horn:
         It was a crest ere thou wast born;
              Thy father's father wore it,   15
              And thy father bore it:
         The horn, the horn, the lusty horn,
         Is not a thing to laugh to scorn.   [*Exeunt*]

---

7. FORESTER Rowe | Lord Ff | 10. SONG | Musicke, Song Ff.—
2 Lord Malone.   FORESTER | Ff omit.

12. The Folios print the words, 'Then sing him home, the rest
shall bear this burthen,' as the third line of the song. Rowe and
Pope followed the Folios; Theobald printed the second half of the
line as a stage direction. In previous editions of Hudson's Shakespeare 'They' was substituted for 'Then,' 'bearing' for 'shall
bear,' and the whole line was bracketed as a stage direction. Knight
gives the music of this song from a curious and rare work, *Catch
that Catch can; or a Choice Collection of Catches, Rounds, &c., col-
lected and published by John Hilton, Batch. in Musicke*, 1652. In
Hilton's arrangement 'Then sing him home' is rejected, but as his
composition is a round for four voices, the omission was perhaps
unavoidable. See Furness for a complete discussion of the "divers
textual arrangements."

SCENE III. *The forest*

Enter ROSALIND *and* CELIA

ROSALIND. How say you now? Is it not past two o'clock?
and here much Orlando !

CELIA. I warrant you, with pure love and troubled brain he
hath ta'en his bow and arrows and is gone forth to sleep.
Look, who comes here.   5

Enter SILVIUS

SILVIUS. My errand is to you, fair youth :
My gentle Phebe bid me give you this :
I know not the contents ; but, as I guess
By the stern brow and waspish action
Which she did use as she was writing of it,   10
It bears an angry tenour : pardon me ;
I am but as a guiltless messenger.

ROSALIND. Patience herself would startle at this letter
And play the swaggerer ; bear this, bear all :
She says I am not fair, that I lack manners ;   15
She calls me proud, and that she could not love me,
Were man as rare as phœnix. 'Od's my will !
Her love is not the hare that I do hunt :
Why writes she so to me? — Well, shepherd, well,
This is a letter of your own device.   20

SILVIUS. No, I protest, I know not the contents :
Phebe did write it.

SCENE III | Scene V Pope.   7. bid F₂F₃F₄ | did bid F₁.
1-5. Printed as verse in Ff.   11. tenour Theobald | tenure Ff.

2. **here much Orlando.** 'Much' is used ironically here ; as we still
say, "A good deal you will," meaning " No, you won't."

ROSALIND.   Come, come, you are a fool,
And turn'd into the extremity of love.
I saw her hand : she has a leathern hand,
A freestone-colour'd hand ; I verily did think   25
That her old gloves were on, but 't was her hands :
She has a huswife's hand ; but that 's no matter.
I say, she never did invent this letter ;
This is a man's invention and his hand.

SILVIUS. Sure, it is hers.   30

ROSALIND. Why, 't is a boisterous and a cruel style,
A style for challengers ; why, she defies me,
Like Turk to Christian : women's gentle brain
Could not drop forth such giant-rude invention,
Such Ethiop words, blacker in their effect   35
Than in their countenance. Will you hear the letter?

SILVIUS. So please you, for I never heard it yet ;
Yet heard too much of Phebe's cruelty.

ROSALIND. She Phebes me : mark how the tyrant writes:

[*Reads*] Art thou god to shepherd turn'd,   40
          That a maiden's heart hath burn'd ? —

Can a woman rail thus?

SILVIUS. Call you this railing?

ROSALIND. [*Reads*]

          Why, thy godhead laid apart,
          Warr'st thou with a woman's heart ? —   45

Did you ever hear such railing ? —

[*Reads*] Whiles the eye of man did woo me,
          That could do no vengeance to me. —

Meaning me a beast. —

[*Reads*] If the scorn of your bright eyne   50
           Have power to raise such love in mine,
           Alack, in me what strange effect
           Would they work in mild aspect!
           Whiles you chid me, I did love;
           How, then, might your prayers move!   55
           He that brings this love to thee
           Little knows this love in me:
           And by him seal up thy mind;
           Whether that thy youth and kind
           Will the faithful offer take   60
           Of me and all that I can make;
           Or else by him my love deny,
           And then I'll study how to die.

SILVIUS. Call you this chiding?

CELIA. Alas, poor shepherd!   65

ROSALIND. Do you pity him? no, he deserves no pity. — Wilt thou love such a woman? What, to make thee an instrument and play false strains upon thee! not to be endur'd! Well, go your way to her, — for I see love hath made thee a tame snake, — and say this to her: That, if she love me, I charge her to love thee; if she will not, I will never have her unless thou entreat for her. If you be a true lover, hence, and not a word; for here comes more company.   [*Exit* SILVIUS]

68. strains F1 | strings F2F3F4.

50. **eyne**: eyes. This form, with the Anglo-Saxon plural ending, is used by Shakespeare nine times, usually in rhymed passages.

58. **And by him seal up thy mind**: seal up your answer and send it back by him.

59. **kind**: nature. Frequently so in Shakespeare.

Enter OLIVER

OLIVER. Good morrow, fair ones : pray you, if you know,
Where in the purlieus of this forest stands   76
A sheep-cote fenc'd about with olive trees?

CELIA. West of this place, down in the neighbour bottom :
The rank of osiers by the murmuring stream
Left on your right hand brings you to the place.   80
But at this hour the house doth keep itself ;
There 's none within.

OLIVER. If that an eye may profit by a tongue,
Then should I know you by description ;
Such garments and such years : ' The boy is fair,   85
Of female favour, and bestows himself
Like a ripe sister ; the woman low,

75. Scene VI Pope.   87. ripe sister Ff | right forester (see
80. brings F₁ | bring F₂F₃F₄.   note). — the F₁ | but the F₂F₃F₄.

75. ones. Wright suggests that we should read ' one,' and Furness
agrees with this suggestion. But in defense of the text it should be
remembered that ' fair ' was often applied to men as well as women
("fair Sir"), and in l. 85 Oliver says, " The boy is fair."

76. purlieus. " Land which had . . . been once forest land and was
afterwards disafforested was known as ' purlieu.' " — *Encyclopædia
Britannica*, IX, 409.

78. bottom : valley. So in *Zechariah*, i, 8 : " the myrtle trees that
were in the bottom."

86. favour: aspect.   See Skeat.   Cf. 'ill-favouredly,' I, ii, 35 ;
'hard-favour'd,' III, iii, 25. — bestows himself: carries himself. Cf.
Two Gentlemen of Verona, III, i, 87.

87. ripe sister. The oddness of this expression and a seeming
defect in the metre led Lettsom to suggest ' right forester ' as an
emendation, and this was adopted in previous editions of Hudson's
Shakespeare. But with ' ripe ' in the sense of ' grown up,' and the
full pause after ' sister ' being equal to a syllable, the Folio reading
becomes intelligible and not unmetrical.

And browner than her brother.' Are not you
The owner of the house I did inquire for?

CELIA. It is no boast, being ask'd, to say we are.   90

OLIVER. Orlando doth commend him to you both;
And to that youth he calls his Rosalind
He sends this bloody napkin. — Are you he?

ROSALIND. I am: what must we understand by this?

OLIVER. Some of my shame; if you will know of me   95
What man I am, and how, and why, and where
This handkercher was stain'd.

CELIA.   I pray you, tell it.

OLIVER. When last the young Orlando parted from you,
He left a promise to return again
Within an hour; and, pacing through the forest,   100
Chewing the food of sweet and bitter fancy,
Lo, what befell! he threw his eye aside,
And mark what object did present itself:
Under an oak, whose boughs were moss'd with age,
And high top bald with dry antiquity   105
A wretched ragged man, o'ergrown with hair,
Lay sleeping on his back: about his neck

---

101. **food** Ff | cud (see note).   104. **an oak** Pope | an old oak Ff.

93. 'Napkin' and 'handkerchief' were often used interchangeably.
'Handkercher,' the form in l. 97, represents a common provincial
pronunciation. "In *Othello* the Quarto reads 'handkercher,' the
Folios 'handkerchief.'" — Clar.

101. **food.** It was Sir Walter Scott (Introduction to *Quentin Dur-
ward*) who first suggested the reading 'cud' adopted by Staunton
and given in previous editions of Hudson's Shakespeare. — **sweet
and bitter.** Malone says that these epithets are in accordance with
the old custom of describing love by contraries. — **fancy:** love. See
note, p. 98, l. 29.

A green and gilded snake had wreath'd itself,
Who with her head, nimble in threats, approach'd
The opening of his mouth ; but suddenly,   110
Seeing Orlando, it unlink'd itself,
And with indented glides did slip away
Into a bush : under which bush's shade
A lioness, with udders all drawn dry,
Lay couching, head on ground, with catlike watch,   115
When that the sleeping man should stir ; for 't is
The royal disposition of that beast
To prey on nothing that doth seem as dead.
This seen, Orlando did approach the man,
And found it was his brother, his elder brother.   120

CELIA.   O, I have heard him speak of that same brother ;
And he did render him the most unnatural
That liv'd amongst men.

OLIVER.   And well he might so do,
For well I know he was unnatural.

ROSALIND.   But, to Orlando : did he leave him there,   125
Food to the suck'd and hungry lioness?

OLIVER. Twice did he turn his back, and purpos'd so ;
But kindness, nobler ever than revenge,
And nature, stronger than his just occasion,
Made him give battle to the lioness,   130

114–118. In Lodge's *Rosalynde* we have : "As thus he lay, a hungry Lyon came hunting downe the edge of the grove for pray, and espying Saladyne began to ceaze upon him : but seeing he lay still without any motion, he left to touch him, for that Lyons hate to pray on dead carkasses ; and yet desirous to have some foode, the Lyon lay downe and watcht to see if he would stirre."

122. render : report, represent, describe. Shakespeare uses 'render' repeatedly in this sense, or in senses akin to this.

Who quickly fell before him : in which hurtling
From miserable slumber I awak'd.

    CELIA. Are you his brother?

    ROSALIND.   Was 't you he rescu'd?

    CELIA. Was 't you that did so oft contrive to kill him?

    OLIVER. 'T was I ; but 't is not I : I do not shame   135
To tell you what I was, since my conversion
So sweetly tastes, being the thing I am.

    ROSALIND. But, for the bloody napkin? —

    OLIVER.   By and by.
When from the first to last betwixt us two
Tears our recountments had most kindly bath'd,   140
As how I came into that desert place ; —
In brief, he led me to the gentle Duke,
Who gave me fresh array and entertainment,
Committing me unto my brother's love ;
Who led me instantly unto his cave,   145
There stripp'd himself ; and here upon his arm
The lioness had torn some flesh away,
Which all this while had bled ; and now he fainted
And cried, in fainting, upon Rosalind.

142. In F₂F₃F₄ | I F₁.

    131. hurtling : jostling or clashing encounter. It is the Middle
English *hurtlen,* a frequentative of *hurten,* ' to dash violently against.'
Chaucer uses the verb transitively :

And he him hurtleth with his hors adoun.

The Knightes Tale, 1758.

In *Julius Cæsar,* II, ii, 22, the verb is used intransitively :

The noise of battle hurtled in the air.

    140. recountments : narratives. Perhaps a Shakespearian coinage
from the verb.

Brief, I recover'd him ; bound up his wound ;   150
And, after some small space, being strong at heart,
He sent me hither, stranger as I am,
To tell this story, that you might excuse
His broken promise ; and to give this napkin,
Dyed in his blood, unto the shepherd youth   155
That he in sport doth call his Rosalind.

    CELIA. Why, how now, Ganymede ! sweet Ganymede !

                        [ROSALIND *swoons*]

    OLIVER. Many will swoon when they do look on blood.

    CELIA. There is more in it. — Cousin Ganymede !

    OLIVER. Look, he recovers.   160

    ROSALIND. I would I were at home.

    CELIA.   We 'll lead you thither. —
I pray you, will you take him by the arm?

    OLIVER. Be of good cheer, youth. You a man ! you lack
a man's heart.   164

    ROSALIND. I do so, I confess it. Ah, sirrah, a body would

---

155. his F2F3F4 | this F1.   it F3F4.—**Cousin Ganymede!** | Cosen
157. [ROSALIND *swoons*] Ff omit.   Ganimed. F1 | Cousin — Ganymede !
In Camb after l. 156.   Johnson.
   159 more in it F1F2 | no more in

155. **his.** " '*This* blood ' is weak compared with ' *his* blood.' That
it is *his* blood, Orlando's very blood, makes Rosalind faint." —
Furness.

159. **Cousin Ganymede.** In previous editions of Hudson's Shakespeare, Johnson's punctuation and his interpretation were adopted :
" Celia, in her first fright, forgets Rosalind's character and disguise, and
calls out ' Cousin,' then recollects herself, and says, ' Ganymede.' "

165. **a body**: a person. The expression is still used colloquially
and in dialect:

> Gin a body meet a body
> Comin' through the rye.

think this was well counterfeited ! I pray you, tell your
brother how well I counterfeited. — Heigh-ho !   167

OLIVER. This was not counterfeit : there is too great
testimony in your complexion that it was a passion of
earnest.

ROSALIND. Counterfeit, I assure you.   171

OLIVER. Well then, take a good heart and counterfeit
to be a man.

ROSALIND. So I do ; but i' faith, I should have been a
woman by right.   175

CELIA. Come, you look paler and paler : pray you, draw
homewards. — Good sir, go with us.

OLIVER. That will I, for I must bear answer back
How you excuse my brother, Rosalind.   179

ROSALIND. I shall devise something : but, I pray you,
commend my counterfeiting to him. — Will you go?

                                        [*Exeunt*]

169. a passion F₁ | passion F₂F₃F₄.

166. Rosalind is afraid of being discovered — that her fainting will
betray her ; and in her anxiety to keep up the show of a saucy, mannish youth, perhaps she slightly overacts the part.

169–170. a passion of earnest : genuine emotion.

ACT V

Scene I. *The forest*

Enter Touchstone *and* Audrey

TOUCHSTONE. We shall find a time, Audrey; patience, gentle Audrey.

AUDREY. Faith, the priest was good enough, for all the old gentleman's saying.   4

TOUCHSTONE. A most wicked Sir Oliver, Audrey, a most vile Martext. But, Audrey, there is a youth here in the forest lays claim to you.   7

AUDREY. Ay, I know who 't is : he hath no interest in me in the world : here comes the man you mean.   9

TOUCHSTONE. It is meat and drink to me to see a clown : by my troth, we that have good wits have much to answer for ; we shall be flouting ; we cannot hold.

Enter William

WILLIAM. Good ev'n, Audrey.   13

AUDREY. God ye good ev'n, William.

Enter Touchstone . . . | Enter Clowne . . . F1.

4. old gentleman's saying. A man mature and of sage speech would readily be called old by a country girl. So nothing certain about the age of Jaques need be based upon Audrey's expression.

12. we shall be flouting: we must be joking. For 'shall' in the sense of 'must,' see Abbott, § 315. — **hold**: restrain or hold in our wits.

14. God ye good ev'n: God give you good even. This is the original salutation in the process of abbreviation into 'good even' or

124

WILLIAM. And good ev'n to you, sir.   15

TOUCHSTONE. Good ev'n, gentle friend. Cover thy head, cover thy head; nay, prithee, be cover'd. How old are you, friend?

WILLIAM. Five and twenty, sir.

TOUCHSTONE. A ripe age. Is thy name William?   20

WILLIAM. William, sir.

TOUCHSTONE. A fair name. Wast born i' the forest here?

WILLIAM. Ay, sir, I thank God.

TOUCHSTONE. 'Thank God'—a good answer. Art rich?

WILLIAM. Faith, sir, so so.   25

TOUCHSTONE. 'So so' is good, very good, very excellent good:—and yet it is not; it is but so so. Art thou wise?

WILLIAM. Ay, sir, I have a pretty wit.   28

TOUCHSTONE. Why, thou say'st well. I do now remember a saying, 'The fool doth think he is wise; but the wise man knows himself to be a fool.' The heathen philosopher, when he had a desire to eat a grape, would open his lips when he put it into his mouth; meaning thereby that grapes were made to eat and lips to open. You do love this maid?   35

WILLIAM. I do, sir.

TOUCHSTONE. Give me your hand. Art thou learned?

'good evening.' In *Romeo and Juliet*, I, ii, 57, 58, the Quartos and Folios print 'Godden' for 'Good even' and 'Godgigoden' for 'God give ye good even.'

17. William is standing with his hat off, in token of respect.

31–35. William may well be supposed to be standing with his mouth agape. One or two of the expressions here have come undoubtedly from Lodge: "Phoebe is no lettice for your lippes, and her grapes hang so high, that gaze at them you may, but touch them you cannot."

WILLIAM. No, sir.   38

TOUCHSTONE. Then learn this of me : to have, is to have ; for it is a figure in rhetoric that drink, being pour'd out of a cup into a glass, by filling the one doth empty the other ; for all your writers do consent that *ipse* is he : now, you are not *ipse*, for I am he.

WILLIAM. Which he, sir?   44

TOUCHSTONE. He, sir, that must marry this woman. Therefore, you clown, abandon, — which is in the vulgar leave, — the society, — which in the boorish is company, — of this female, — which in the common is woman ; which together is, abandon the society of this female ; or, clown, thou perishest ; or, to thy better understanding, diest ; or, to wit, I kill thee, make thee away, translate thy life into death, thy liberty into bondage. I will deal in poison with thee, or in bastinado, or in steel ; I will bandy with thee in faction ; I will o'er-run thee with policy ; I will kill thee a hundred and fifty ways : therefore tremble, and depart.   55

AUDREY. Do, good William.

WILLIAM. God rest you merry, sir.   [*Exit*]

Enter CORIN

CORIN. Our master and mistress seeks you ; come, away, away !   59

TOUCHSTONE. Trip, Audrey ! trip, Audrey ! I attend, I attend.   [*Exeunt*]

---

54. **policy** F₂F₃F₄ | police F₁.   57. **merry,** F₄ | merry F₁F₂F₃.

53–54. **bandy with thee in faction** : beat you backwards and forwards by means of conspiracy. — 54. **policy** : stratagem.

57. **rest you merry** : keep you merry, continue happiness to you. This was a common Elizabethan form of farewell.

SCENE II. *The forest*

Enter ORLANDO *and* OLIVER

ORLANDO. Is 't possible that on so little acquaintance you should like her? that but seeing you should love her? and loving woo? and, wooing, she should grant? and will you persever to enjoy her?   4

OLIVER. Neither call the giddiness of it in question, the poverty of her, the small acquaintance, my sudden wooing, nor her sudden consenting; but say with me, I love Aliena; say with her that she loves me; consent with both that we may enjoy each other: it shall be to your good; for my father's house, and all the revenue that was old Sir Rowland's, will I estate upon you, and here live and die a shepherd.   11

ORLANDO. You have my consent. Let your wedding be to-morrow: thither will I invite the Duke and all 's contented followers. Go you and prepare Aliena; for look you, here comes my Rosalind.   15

Enter ROSALIND

ROSALIND. God save you, brother.

OLIVER. And you, fair sister.   [*Exit*]

4. **persever** F1F2 | persevere F3F4.   12-15. Printed as verse in Ff.
7. **nor her** Rowe | nor Ff.   17. OLIVER | Ol. F1 | Orl. F3F4.

4. **persever.** Always so spelled in Shakespeare, down to the publication of the Third Folio, except, as Schmidt notes, in the Quartos of *King Lear*. It was accented on the second syllable.

11. **estate**: settle, bestow. Cf. *The Tempest*, IV, i, 85.

17. Oliver has before this learned from Celia the whole secret of who Ganymede and Aliena are. Hence he calls Rosalind 'sister' here, well knowing that Orlando will understand him as referring to the character she is sustaining in her masked courtship.

ROSALIND. O, my dear Orlando, how it grieves me to see thee wear thy heart in a scarf!

ORLANDO. It is my arm.   20

ROSALIND. I thought thy heart had been wounded with the claws of a lion.

ORLANDO. Wounded it is, but with the eyes of a lady.

ROSALIND. Did your brother tell you how I counterfeited to swoon when he show'd me your handkercher?   25

ORLANDO. Ay, and greater wonders than that.

ROSALIND. O, I know where you are : — nay, 't is true : there was never any thing so sudden but the fight of two rams, and Cæsar's thrasonical brag of — 'I came, saw, and overcame' : for your brother and my sister no sooner met but they look'd ; no sooner look'd but they lov'd ; no sooner lov'd but they sigh'd ; no sooner sigh'd but they ask'd one another the reason ; no sooner knew the reason but they sought the remedy : and in these degrees have they made a pair of stairs to marriage which they will climb incontinent : they are in the very wrath of love and they will together ; clubs cannot part them.   37

---

25. swoon Rowe | sound F₁F₂F₃ | swound F₄.

28. fight F₁F₂F₃ | sight F₄.

30. overcame F₂F₃F₄ | overcome F₁.

29. thrasonical. From Thraso, the name of a bragging, vainglorious soldier in the *Eunuchus* of Terence. — 29–30. I came, saw, and overcame. Shakespeare's unvarying translation (as in *Cymbeline*, III, i, 24 ; *Love's Labour's Lost*, IV, i, 70 ; *2 Henry IV*, IV, iii, 46) of *Veni, vidi, vici*, Cæsar's famous dispatch to the Roman Senate.

36. incontinent : immediately. So in *Othello*, IV, iii, 12.

37. ' Clubs, clubs ! ' was the rallying cry of the 'prentices in Elizabethan London when a street fray broke out (see Scott, *The Fortunes of Nigel*, Chapter I). They were not allowed to carry swords and used to quell (sometimes raise) such disturbances with their ' crabtree staves.' Cf. *Titus Andronicus*, II, i, 37 ; *Henry VIII*, V, iv, 53.

ORLANDO. They shall be married to-morrow, and I will bid the Duke to the nuptial. But, O, how bitter a thing it is to look into happiness through another man's eyes! By so much the more shall I to-morrow be at the height of heart-heaviness, by how much I shall think my brother happy in having what he wishes for. 43

ROSALIND. Why then, to-morrow I cannot serve your turn for Rosalind?

ORLANDO. I can live no longer by thinking. 46

ROSALIND. I will weary you, then, no longer with idle talking. Know of me then, for now I speak to some purpose, that I know you are a gentleman of good conceit: I speak not this, that you should bear a good opinion of my knowledge, insomuch I say I know you are; neither do I labour for a greater esteem than may in some little measure draw a belief from you, to do yourself good and not to grace me. Believe, then, if you please, that I can do strange things: I have, since I was three year old, convers'd with a magician, most profound in his art and yet not damnable. If you do love Rosalind so near the heart as your gesture cries it out, when your brother marries Aliena, shall you marry her: I know into what straits of

56. art F1 | heart F3F4.   59. shall you F1F2 | you shall F3F4.

49. conceit: sense, judgment, understanding. This word is used by Shakespeare of all the forms of mental action and always in a good sense. 'Wit' is also used by the Elizabethan writers with a similar largeness of meaning.

57. damnable: meriting punishment. By an Elizabethan statute the practice of magic was held to be criminal and was punishable with death. Rosalind means that her preceptor, though a magician, used magic only for honest and charitable ends; such a pure and benevolent magician, perhaps, as Shakespeare revealed in Prospero.

fortune she is driven; and it is not impossible to me, if it appear not inconvenient to you, to set her before your eyes to-morrow, human as she is, and without any danger.   62

ORLANDO. Speak'st thou in sober meanings?

ROSALIND. By my life, I do; which I tender dearly, though I say I am a magician. Therefore, put you in your best array; bid your friends; for, if you will be married to-morrow, you shall; and to Rosalind, if you will.   67

Enter SILVIUS *and* PHEBE

Look, here comes a lover of mine and a lover of hers.

PHEBE. Youth, you have done me much ungentleness, To show the letter that 'I writ to you.   70

ROSALIND. I care not if I have; it is my study To seem despiteful and ungentle to you. You are there follow'd by a faithful shepherd: Look upon him, love him; he worships you.   74

PHEBE. Good shepherd, tell this youth what 't is to love.

SILVIUS. It is to be all made of sighs and tears; And so am I for Phebe.

PHEBE. And I for Ganymede.

ORLANDO. And I for Rosalind.

ROSALIND. And I for no woman.   80

---

62. **human** Rowe | humane Ff.   76. **all made** F₁F₂ | made all F₃
69. Scene III Pope.   F₄.

61–62. That is, as Johnson remarked, Rosalind her very self, and not a mere phantom of her, conjured up by magic rites, such as it was dangerous to practice.

64. **tender dearly:** value highly. Rosalind alludes to the danger in which her avowal of practicing magic, had it been serious, would have involved her.

SILVIUS. It is to be all made of faith and service;
And so am I for Phebe.

PHEBE. And I for Ganymede.

ORLANDO. And I for Rosalind.

ROSALIND. And I for no woman.   85

SILVIUS. It is to be all made of fantasy,
All made of passion, and all made of wishes;
All adoration, duty, and observance,
All humbleness, all patience and impatience,
All purity, all trial, all observance;   90
And so am I for Phebe.

PHEBE. And so am I for Ganymede.

ORLANDO. And so am I for Rosalind.

ROSALIND. And so am I for no woman.

PHEBE. If this be so, why blame you me to love you? 95

SILVIUS. If this be so, why blame you me to love you?

ORLANDO. If this be so, why blame you me to love you?

ROSALIND. Why do you speak too, 'Why blame you me
to love you?'

---

90. **observance** Ff | obedience Ma-
lone conj. | endurance Harness conj.
| devotion Bailey conj.

98. **Why ... too** F1 | Who ... to
Rowe | Whom ... to Singer.

90. **observance.** The textual notes show the conjectural emendations for this second 'observance,' which most editors regard as an
error. Furness favors 'obedience'; in previous editions of Hudson's
Shakespeare 'endurance' was adopted.

95. **to love you**: for loving you. The indefinite, gerundive use of
the infinitive (Abbott, § 356).

98. **Why do you speak too.** Rowe corrected this to 'Who do you
speak to,' and this reading was adopted in previous editions of Hudson's Shakespeare on the ground that the next speech proves the
First Folio reading to be wrong. Furness says, "I cannot see the
trace of a sufficient reason for deserting the Folio."

ORLANDO. To her that is not here, nor doth not hear. 100

ROSALIND. Pray you, no more of this; 't is like the howling of Irish wolves against the moon. — [*To* SILVIUS] I will
help you, if I can : — [*To* PHEBE] I would love you, if I
could. — To-morrow meet me all together. — [*To* PHEBE]
I will marry you, if ever I marry woman, and I 'll be married to-morrow : — [*To* ORLANDO] I will satisfy you, if ever
I satisfied man, and you shall be married to-morrow : —
[*To* SILVIUS] I will content you, if what pleases you contents you, and you shall be married to-morrow. — [*To*
ORLANDO] As you love Rosalind, meet : — [*To* SILVIUS] As
you love Phebe, meet : and as I love no woman, I 'll meet.
— So, fare you well : I have left you commands.   112

SILVIUS. I 'll not fail, if I live.

PHEBE. Nor I.

ORLANDO. Nor I.   [*Exeunt*]

102-110. [*To* SILVIUS], [*To* PHEBE],   104. all together F₄ | altogether
etc. | no stage directions in Ff.   F₁F₂F₃.

102. The suggestion is that this howling of 'Irish wolves' is
monotonous and dismal. Malone traces a connection between the
expression and this sentence from Lodge : "I tell thee, Montanus,
in courting Phœbe thou barkest with the wolves of Syria against the
moone." But, as Furness says, " It is a far cry, or, rather, a far 'bark,'
from Syria to Ireland." Caldecott, too, points out that the two
phrases are dissimilar in meaning. Wright states that wolves held
their ground in Ireland until a recent period ; it was the last of the
British Islands to harbor the ancient British wolf, and he quotes the
following from Spenser's *A View of the Present State of Ireland* :
"Also the Scythians sayd, that they were once every yeare turned
into wolves, and soe is it written of the Irish : though Mr. Camden
in a better sence doth suppose it was a disease, called Lycanthropia,
so named of the wolfe. And yet some of the Irish doe use to make
the wolfe theyr gossip."

SCENE III. *The forest*

Enter TOUCHSTONE *and* AUDREY

TOUCHSTONE. To-morrow is the joyful day, Audrey ; to-morrow will we be married.

AUDREY. I do desire it with all my heart; and I hope it is no dishonest desire to desire to be a woman of the world. Here come two of the banish'd Duke's pages.   5

Enter two Pages

FIRST PAGE. Well met, honest gentleman.

TOUCHSTONE. By my troth, well met. Come, sit, sit, and a song.

SECOND PAGE. We are for you : sit i' the middle.   9

FIRST PAGE. Shall we clap into 't roundly, without hawking, or spitting, or saying we are hoarse, which are the only prologues to a bad voice?   12

SECOND PAGE. I' faith, i' faith ; and both in a tune, like two gipsies on a horse.

SCENE III | Scene IV Pope.—   5. world. F_4 | world ? $F_1F_2F_3$.
TOUCHSTONE | Clowne F_1.   11. the only Ff | only the Capell conj.

4. **dishonest** : immodest. Cf. 'honest' in I, ii, 34 ; III, iii, 22. Ben Jonson described his wife to Drummond of Hawthornden as "a shrew, yet honest." — 4–5. **to be a woman of the world** : to be married. To be 'a woman of the world' is opposed to being 'a woman of the Church,' which implied a vow of perpetual celibacy. Cf. *Much Ado About Nothing*, II, i, 330 ; *All 's Well that Ends Well*, I, iii, 19–20.

10. **clap into 't roundly** : strike into it directly. So in *Measure for Measure*, IV, iii, 43.

11. **the only** : only the. So in I, ii, 171, where "only . . . I fill" should be "I only fill." For this transposition of 'only,' see Abbott, § 420.

SONG

It was a lover and his lass,   15
    With a hey, and a ho, and a hey nonino,
That o'er the green corn-field did pass
    In the spring time, the only pretty ring time,
When birds do sing, hey ding a' ding, ding :
Sweet lovers love the Spring.   20

Between the acres of the rye,
    With a hey, and a ho, and a hey nonino,
These pretty country folks would lie
    In spring time, etc.

This carol they began that hour,   25
    With a hey, and a ho, and a hey nonino,
How that a life was but a flower
    In spring time, etc.

---

18. **ring time** | rang time Ff.   25. **This** F_1F_2 | The F_3F_4.
24, 28. In F_1F_2 | In the F_3F_4.

15. **It was a lover and his lass.** Probably suggested by the song sung by Lodge's Corydon at the wedding feast :

> A blythe and bonny country Lasse,
> Heigh ho the bonny Lasse.

16. **hey nonino.** With reference to these "meaningless burdens of songs" Wright quotes the following from Coverdale's Preface to his *Ghostly Psalms :* "And if women, sitting at their rocks, or spinning at the wheels, had none other songs to pass their time withal, than such as Moses' sister, Glehana's [Elkanah's] wife, Debora, and Mary the mother of Christ, have sung before them, they should be better occupied than with hey nony nony, hey troly loly, and such like phantasies."

18. **ring time.** Probably the season for exchanging rings, the marriage time, but it may have reference to what Nash describes in the second line of his famous spring lyric, — "then maids dance in a ring."

> And therefore take the present time,
>> With a hey, and a ho, and a hey nonino;   30
> For love is crowned with the prime
>> In spring time, etc.

TOUCHSTONE. Truly, young gentlemen, though there was
no great matter in the ditty, yet the note was very untuneable.   35

FIRST PAGE. You are deceiv'd, sir: we kept time, we lost
not our time.   37

TOUCHSTONE. By my troth, yes; I count it but time lost
to hear such a foolish song. God be wi' you; and God
mend your voices! — Come, Audrey.   [*Exeunt*]

SCENE IV. *The forest*

Enter DUKE SENIOR, AMIENS, JAQUES, ORLANDO, OLIVER,
and CELIA

DUKE SENIOR. Dost thou believe, Orlando, that the boy
Can do all this that he hath promised?

29-32. Placed after l. 19 in Ff.   39. **be wi'** | buy Ff.
34-35. **untuneable** Ff | untimeable   SCENE IV | Scene V Pope.
Theobald.

29. In the Folios this is the second stanza. Thirlby suggested and
Johnson made the transposition now generally accepted — a transposition found too in a valuable seventeenth century manuscript version of the song in the Advocates' Library, Edinburgh.

34. **matter**: sense, meaning. — 34-35. **untuneable**. For this Theobald substituted 'untimeable,' but 'tune' and 'time' were formerly
almost synonymous. Wright suggests that Theobald forgot that
Touchstone is the speaker. "The page misunderstands him in order
to give him an opening for another joke." — Clar.

39. **God be wi' you**. See note, p. 79, l. 244.

ORLANDO. I sometimes do believe, and sometimes do not;
As those that fear they hope, and know they fear.   4

Enter ROSALIND, SILVIUS, *and* PHEBE

ROSALIND. Patience once more, whiles our compact is
    urg'd. —
You say, if I bring in your Rosalind,
You will bestow her on Orlando here?   7
    DUKE SENIOR. That would I, had I kingdoms to give
        with her.
    ROSALIND. And you say, you will have her, when I bring her?
    ORLANDO. That would I, were I of all kingdoms king. 10
    ROSALIND. You say, you 'll marry me, if I be willing?
    PHEBE. That will I, should I die the hour after.
    ROSALIND. But if you do refuse to marry me,
You 'll give yourself to this most faithful shepherd?
    PHEBE. So is the bargain.   15
    ROSALIND. You say, that you 'll have Phebe, if she will?
    SILVIUS. Though to have her and death were both one
        thing.
    ROSALIND. I 've promis'd to make all this matter even.
Keep you your word, O Duke, to give your daughter; —
You yours, Orlando, to receive his daughter: —   20
Keep your word, Phebe, that you 'll marry me,

14. **shepherd?** Capell | Shepheard. Ff.   21. **your** Rowe | you your Ff.

4. Many emendations (see Furness) have been suggested for this
reading of the Folios. The general meaning is clear: As those that
fear lest they may believe a thing because they wish it true, and at
the same time know that this fear is no better ground of action than
their hope. Who has not sometime caught himself in a similar per-
plexity of hope and fear?

Or else refusing me, to wed this shepherd : —
Keep your word, Silvius, that you 'll marry her,
If she refuse me : — and from hence I go,
To make these doubts all even.   25

                   [*Exeunt* ROSALIND *and* CELIA]

DUKE SENIOR. I do remember in this shepherd boy
Some lively touches of my daughter's favour.

ORLANDO. My lord, the first time that I ever saw him
Methought he was a brother to your daughter :
But, my good lord, this boy is forest-born,   30
And hath been tutor'd in the rudiments
Of many desperate studies by his uncle,
Whom he reports to be a great magician,
Obscured in the circle of this forest.   34

Enter TOUCHSTONE *and* AUDREY

JAQUES. There is, sure, another flood toward, and these
couples are coming to the ark. Here comes a pair of very
strange beasts, which in all tongues are call'd fools.   37

TOUCHSTONE. Salutation and greeting to you all !

JAQUES. Good my lord, bid him welcome : this is the

---

26. shepherd F₁F₂F₃ | shepherds   *Enter* TOUCHSTONE . . . | Enter
F₄.   Clowne and Audrey Ff (after l. 33).
    35. Scene VI Pope.

    27. favour : aspect, look. See note, p. 118, l. 86.
    29. This shows the danger Rosalind has been in of being dis-
covered, notwithstanding her disguise. Doubtless we have all found
how one face will sometimes remind us of another by tricks of asso-
ciation too subtle for our tracing, so that we seem at the same time
to know and not to know the stranger.
    38. Touchstone affects the manners and language of the court.

motley-minded gentleman that I have so often met in the
forest : he hath been a courtier, he swears.   41

TOUCHSTONE. If any man doubt that, let him put me to
my purgation. I have trod a measure ; I have flatter'd a
lady ; I have been politic with my friend, smooth with mine
enemy ; I have undone three tailors ; I have had four
quarrels, and like to have fought one.   46

JAQUES. And how was that ta'en up?

TOUCHSTONE. Faith, we met, and found the quarrel was
upon the seventh cause.   49

JAQUES. How seventh cause? — Good my lord, like this
fellow.

DUKE SENIOR. I like him very well.   52

---

44. been F4 | bin F1F2F3.   50. seventh F1F2 | the seventh F3F4.

42-43. put me to my purgation : make me swear to the truth of
the matter. See note, p. 29, l. 49. People were often called upon
or permitted to 'purge' or clear themselves of imputed guilt by
thus affirming their innocence under oath. Sometimes a man got
others to swear with him, and these were called compurgators. —
43. a measure. The 'measure' was a grave, solemn dance, with a
slow and measured step, somewhat like a minuet, and therefore well
comporting with the dignity of the court.

44-45. Touchstone implies that to use sharp practice on one's
friend, to cajole and beguile one's enemy, and to bankrupt one's
tailors by running up huge accounts and leaving them unpaid, are
characteristics of courts and courtiers.

47. ta'en up : made up. So in *Twelfth Night*, III, iv, 320.

49. seventh cause. This means, apparently, that the quarrel had
proceeded through six degrees from the original ground or starting
point, and so had come to the seventh degree, the " Lie Direct,"
where nothing but an ' if ' could save the parties from the necessity
of fighting it out. In *Romeo and Juliet*, II, iv, 26, Tybalt is described as " a gentleman of the very first house, — of the first and
second cause"; that is, one who will fight on the slightest provocation.

TOUCHSTONE. God 'ild you, sir; I desire you of the like.
I press in here, sir, amongst the rest of the country copulatives, to swear and to forswear, according as marriage binds
and blood breaks. A poor virgin, sir, an ill-favour'd thing,
sir, but mine own; a poor humour of mine, sir, to take that
that no man else will: rich honesty dwells like a miser, sir,
in a poor house; as your pearl in your foul oyster.   59

DUKE SENIOR. By my faith, he is very swift and sententious.

TOUCHSTONE. According to the fool's bolt, sir, and such
dulcet diseases.   62

JAQUES. But, for the seventh cause; how did you find
the quarrel on the seventh cause?   64

TOUCHSTONE. Upon a lie seven times remov'd; — bear
your body more seeming, Audrey; — as thus, sir: I did

---

59. **foul** omitted in F₃F₄.   62. **diseases** | discourses Johnson conj.

53. **God 'ild you:** God yield you, God reward you. So in III, iii,
66. — **I desire you of the like:** I wish you the same.
54–55. **copulatives.** A word coined by Touchstone to describe
people wishing to be married.
56. **blood:** passion. It connotes impulse, as opposed to reason.
57. **but mine own.** Touchstone here just hits the very pith of the
matter. It is by such strokes as this that Shakespeare keeps the man,
fool though he be, bound up fresh and warm with our human sympathies. Celia gives the keynote of his real, inside character, when
she says, "He 'll go along o'er the wide world with me."
59. **your.** The personal pronouns were often used thus in an
indefinite sense of what is well known. So in III, ii, 52.
60. **swift:** quick-witted. — **sententious:** full of pithy sayings.
61. **bolt:** a short, thick, blunt arrow for shooting near objects.
It required little practice or skill. Cf. *Henry V*, III, vii, 132: "A
fool's bolt is soon shot."
62. **dulcet diseases.** The sense of this probably lies in the circumstance of its being meant for what Barrow calls "acute nonsense."
66. **seeming:** seemingly. The adjective for the adverb.

dislike the cut of a certain courtier's beard : he sent me word, if I said his beard was not cut well, he was in the mind it was : this is call'd the Retort Courteous. If I sent him word again, 'it was not well cut,' he would send me word, he cut it to please himself : this is call'd the Quip Modest. If again, 'it was not well cut,' he disabl'd my judgment : this is call'd the Reply Churlish. If again, 'it was not well cut,' he would answer, I spake not true : this is call'd the Reproof Valiant. If again, 'it was not well cut,' he would say, I lie : this is call'd the Countercheck Quarrelsome : and so to the Lie Circumstantial and the Lie Direct.   77

JAQUES. And how oft did you say his beard was not well cut?   79

TOUCHSTONE. I durst go no further than the Lie Circumstantial, nor he durst not give me the Lie Direct ; and so we measur'd swords, and parted.   82

JAQUES. Can you nominate in order now the degrees of the lie?   84

TOUCHSTONE. O sir, we quarrel in print, by the book ; as you have books for good manners : I will name you the degrees. The first, the Retort Courteous ; the second, the Quip Modest ; the third, the Reply Churlish ; the fourth,

---

76. lie Ff | lied Hanmer.   77. so to the F₂F₃F₄ | so ro F₁.

72. disabl'd : disparaged, disqualified. So in IV, i, 31.

85. by the book. Warburton first suggested that 'the book' referred to is a fantastic treatise on dueling by one Vincentio Saviolo, printed in 1594–1595, but Furness thinks that, if Shakespeare had any particular book in view, it may just as likely have been *The Book of Honor and Arms, wherein is discoursed the Causes of Quarrell, and the nature of Iniuries, with their Repulses, &c.* (1590).

86. books for good manners. The sixteenth century saw the publication of several treatises on etiquette.

the Reproof Valiant; the fifth, the Countercheck Quarrel-some; the sixth, the Lie with Circumstance; the seventh, the Lie Direct. All these you may avoid, but the Lie Direct; and you may avoid that too with an If. I knew when seven justices could not take up a quarrel; but when the parties were met themselves, one of them thought but of an If, as 'If you said so, then I said so'; and they shook hands, and swore brothers. Your If is the only peace-maker; much virtue in If. 97

JAQUES. Is not this a rare fellow, my lord? he's as good at any thing, and yet a fool.

DUKE SENIOR. He uses his folly like a stalking-horse, and under the presentation of that he shoots his wit. 101

Enter HYMEN, ROSALIND, *and* CELIA

Still Music

HYMEN.   Then is there mirth in heaven,
            When earthly things made even   103
            Atone together. —

102. Scene VII Pope.   ROSALIND | Rosalind in Woman's
                                        Clothes Rowe.

100. **a stalking-horse.** "A horse, either real or fictitious, by which the fowler anciently sheltered himself from the sight of the game." — Steevens. The 'fictitious' horse was usually a piece of stretched canvas with a horse painted on it.

102. **HYMEN.** Rosalind is imagined by the rest of the company to be brought by enchantment, and is introduced by a supposed aërial being in the character of Hymen. The masque in *The Tempest* resembles this, and is similarly accompanied by soft, or 'still,' music.

104. **atone together**: are at one. The Folio spelling 'attone' has led to the conjecture that 'attune' should be read here. The verb 'atone' does not occur in the Bible (King James version).

Good Duke, receive thy daughter :   105
Hymen from heaven brought her,
   Yea, brought her hither,
That thou mightst join her hand with his
Whose heart within his bosom is.   109

ROSALIND. [*To the* DUKE] To you I give myself, for I
   am yours. —
[*To* ORLANDO] To you I give myself, for I am yours.
DUKE SENIOR. If there be truth in sight, you are my
   daughter.   112
ORLANDO. If there be truth in sight, you are my Rosalind.
PHEBE. If sight and shape be true,
Why, then, — my love adieu !   115
ROSALIND. [*To the* DUKE] I 'll have no father, if you be
   not he : —
[*To* ORLANDO] I 'll have no husband, if you be not he : —
[*To* PHEBE] Nor ne'er wed woman, if you be not she.
HYMEN. Peace, ho ! I bar confusion :
   'T is I must make conclusion   120
   Of these most strange events :
   Here 's eight that must take hands
   To join in Hymen's bands,
   If truth holds true contents. —

107. hither F3F4 | hether F1F2.   109. his Ff | her Malone.
108. her hand F3F4 | his hand F1F2. 114-115. Ff print as one line.

109. his. Almost all modern editors adopt Malone's emendation
'her'; but if we take 'her' in the preceding line as the antecedent
of 'whose,' the Folio reading becomes intelligible.

110. Rowe, Pope, and Johnson introduced the stage directions in
this scene.

124. If there be truth in truth itself. " If truth contains truth."

[*To* ORLANDO *and* ROSALIND] You and you no cross shall
   part : ——   125
[*To* OLIVER *and* CELIA] You and you are heart in heart : ——
[*To* PHEBE] You to his love must accord,
   Or have a woman to your lord : ——
[*To* TOUCHSTONE *and* AUDREY] You and you are sure together,
   As the winter to foul weather.   130
   Whiles a wedlock-hymn we sing,
   Feed yourselves with questioning ;
   That reason wonder may diminish,
   How thus we met, and these things finish.

       SONG

   Wedding is great Juno's crown :   135
     O blessed bond of board and bed !
   'T is Hymen peoples every town ;
     High wedlock, then, be honoured :
   Honour, high honour, and renown,
   To Hymen, god of every town !   140

DUKE SENIOR. O my dear niece, welcome thou art to me,
Even daughter, welcome, in no less degree !
  PHEBE. [*To* SILVIUS] I will not eat my word, now thou
   art mine ;
Thy faith my fancy to thee doth combine.   144

---

 142. **daughter, welcome** F4 | welcome Theobald.
daughter welcome, F1F2F3 | daughter- 143. [*To* SILVIUS] Capell.

 132. **questioning** : conversation. So with 'question' in l. 155.
 142. The variations in punctuation indicated in the textual notes
do not make any essential difference in the meaning — 'welcome as
a daughter equally with Rosalind.'
 144. **combine** : bind. So in *Measure for Measure*, IV, iii, 149.

Enter JAQUES DE BOYS

JAQUES DE BOYS. Let me have audience for a word or two :
I am the second son of old Sir Rowland,   146
That bring these tidings to this fair assembly :
Duke Frederick, hearing how that every day
Men of great worth resorted to this forest,
Address'd a mighty power ; which were on foot,   150
In his own conduct, purposely to take
His brother here and put him to the sword :
And to the skirts of this wild wood he came ;
Where meeting with an old religious man,
After some question with him, was converted   155
Both from his enterprise and from the world ;
His crown bequeathing to his banish'd brother,
And all their lands restor'd to them again
That were with him exil'd. This to be true,
I do engage my life.

DUKE SENIOR.   Welcome, young man ;   160
Thou offer'st fairly to thy brothers' wedding :
To one his lands withheld ; and to the other
A land itself at large, a potent dukedom.
First, in this forest let us do those ends

---

145. Scene VIII Pope.   158. **them** Rowe | him Ff.
     Enter JAQUES DE BOYS | Enter   161. **brothers'** Capell | brothers
Second Brother Ff.   F₁F₂F₃.

150. **Address'd** : prepared, made ready, as in *Henry V*, III, iii, 58.
151. **In his own conduct** : under his own command.
162. The ' one ' is Oliver, whose lands had been seized by Frederick ; ' the other ' is Orlando, who with Rosalind is to inherit the
dukedom, she being the old Duke's only child. The sense of
' offer'st ' is continued through these two lines.

That here were well begun and well begot ;   165
And after, every of this happy number,
That have endur'd shrewd days and nights with us,
Shall share the good of our returned fortune,
According to the measure of their states.
Meantime forget this new-fall'n dignity,   170
And fall into our rustic revelry. —
Play, music ! — and you, brides and bridegrooms all,
With measure heap'd in joy, to th' measures fall.

JAQUES. Sir, by your patience. — If I heard you rightly,
The Duke hath put on a religious life,   175
And thrown into neglect the pompous court?

JAQUES DE BOYS. He hath.

JAQUES. To him will I : out of these convertites
There is much matter to be heard and learn'd. —   179
[*To* DUKE SENIOR] You to your former honour I bequeath ;
Your patience and your virtue well deserves it : —
[*To* ORLANDO] You to a love that your true faith doth
              merit : —   182
[*To* OLIVER] You to your land, and love, and great allies : —

180-185. [*To* DUKE SENIOR], [*To*   181. deserves Ff | deserve Pope.
ORLANDO], etc. Rowe | not given in Ff.

167. shrewd: sharp, bitter. " The air bites shrewdly." The root-
notion of 'biting' still survives in 'shrew-mouse.' In Chaucer the
adjective *shrewd* means 'evil,' 'accursed,' while the noun *shrewe*
means a 'scoundrel' as well as an 'ill-natured person.'

169. states: estates. In Shakespeare the two words are used
interchangeably, as in *The Merchant of Venice*, III, ii, 239, 262.

175. put on a religious life. This probably should be taken literally in the sense of having put on a monk's or hermit's dress —
the badge of a religious life.

176. pompous : ceremonious. This is the true, original meaning.

178. convertites: converts. Cf. *King John*, V, i, 19.

[*To* SILVIUS] You to a long and well-deserved bed : —
[*To* TOUCHSTONE] And you to wrangling; for thy loving
                    voyage   185
Is but for two months victuall'd. — So, to your pleasures :
I am for other than for dancing measures.

    DUKE SENIOR. Stay, Jaques, stay.

    JAQUES. To see no pastime I : what you would have 189
I 'll stay to know at your abandon'd cave.   [*Exit*]

    DUKE SENIOR. Proceed, proceed : we will begin these rites,
As we do trust they 'll end, in true delights.   [*A dance*]

EPILOGUE

    ROSALIND. It is not the fashion to see the lady the epi-
logue; but it is no more unhandsome than to see the lord
the prologue. If it be true that good wine needs no bush,
't is true that a good play needs no epilogue : yet to good
wine they do use good bushes; and good plays prove the
better by the help of good epilogues. What a case am I in
then, that am neither a good epilogue, nor cannot insinuate
with you in the behalf of a good play ! I am not furnish'd
like a beggar, therefore to beg will not become me : my
way is to conjure you ; and I 'll begin with the women. I
charge you, O women, for the love you bear to men, to like
as much of this play as please you : and I charge you, O

191. rites Rowe | rights Ff.   12. please F₁F₂ | pleases F₃F₄.

    EPILOGUE. Theobald was the first to print this as an epilogue.
Seymour regarded what follows as spurious.

    3. A bush of ivy was in old England a common vintner's sign, ivy
being sacred to Bacchus. So in Nash's *Summer's Last Will and
Testament :* "Green ivy-bushes at the vintners' doors."

men, for the love you bear to women, (as I perceive by your simpering, none of you hates them,) that between you and the women the play may please. If I were a woman, I would kiss as many of you as had beards that pleas'd me, complexions that lik'd me and breaths that I defied not : and, I am sure, as many as have good beards or good faces or sweet breaths will, for my kind offer, when I make curtsy, bid me farewell.   [*Exeunt*]

14. **hates** Ff | hate Pope.   20. [*Exeunt*] F2F3F4 | Exit F1.

15. **If I were a woman.** This epilogue was spoken in his own person by the youth who had acted the part of Rosalind. The parts of women were taken by men or boys in Shakespeare's time. Women did not appear on the public stage until after the Restoration, though there is clear enough evidence that they had acted often before 1660 in masques and private dramatic performances.

17. **lik'd** : pleased. So in *The Two Gentlemen of Verona*, IV, ii, 56. — **defied** : disliked, repudiated. So in *King John*, III, iv, 23.

INDEX

This Index includes the most important words, phrases, etc., explained in the notes. The figures in heavy-faced type refer to the pages; those in plain type, to the lines containing what is explained.

Act I

Scene I   Orchard of Oliver's house
  "   II.   Lawn before the Duke's palace
       III   A room in the palace.

       Act. II
Scene I . The Forest of Arden.
       II   A room in the palace.
       III   Before Oliver's house
       IV   Forest of Arden .
       V .   The forest
       VI.   The forest — Orlando , Adam
       VII   The forest — Duke , Amiens

       Act III
Scene I   A room in the palace
       II   The forest
       III   The forest
       IV   The forest   Rosalind & Celia